Essentials of
Accounting

Eighth Edition

Robert N. Anthony and Leslie Pearlman Breitner

Harvard Business School   *Harvard Kennedy School of Government*

University of Washington, Evans School of Public Affairs

Prentice
Hall

Upper Saddle River, New Jersey 07458

for Katherine (RNA)
for JCSB (LB)

Library of Congress Cataloguing-in-Publication data is available.

Executive Editor: Deborah Hoffman
Editor-in-Chief: P. J. Boardman
Editorial Assistant: Jane Avery
Executive Marketing Manager: Beth Toland
Marketing Assistant: Christine Genneken
Managing Editor: John Roberts
Permissions Coordinator: Suzanne Grappi
Associate Director, Manufacturing: Vincent Scelta
Production Manager: Arnold Vila
Manufacturing Buyer: Michelle Klein
Cover Design: Blair Brown
Cover Photo: Eric Perlman/Corbis Stock Market
Composition, Full-Service Project Management: Carlisle Communications
Printer/Binder: Courier–Stoughton

Pearson Education LTD.
Pearson Education Australia PTY, Limited
Pearson Education Singapore, Pte. Ltd
Pearson Education North Asia Ltd
Pearson Education, Canada, Ltd
Pearson Educación de Mexico, S.A. de C.V.
Pearson Education–Japan
Pearson Education Malaysia, Pte. Ltd

10 9 8 7 6
ISBN 0-13-040672-4

Contents

The following are in a separate booklet attached to the back of the book.

Exhibits

Post Tests

Answers to Post Tests

Glossary and Index

Introduction

This book will help you teach yourself the essential ideas of accounting. You will learn what accounting information can—and cannot—tell you about an organization.

Accounting is the principal way of organizing and reporting financial information. Although there are differences in detail, the general structure and rules are similar in most countries and in most types of organizations.

Accounting has been called the language of business. Learning this language is complicated by the fact that many words used in accounting do not mean quite the same thing as they mean in everyday life. When using accounting words, it is important that you understand their accounting meaning.

As in any language, some accounting rules and terms have a single correct meaning, and others are like dialects in that their meaning varies with different users. You will learn to understand and allow for these differences.

HOW TO USE THIS PROGRAM

This program consists of "frames." Each frame asks you to DO something: answer a question, make a calculation, fill in blanks. But these frames are NOT tests. As in most learning experiences, you learn by doing. You should be able to complete most frames without difficulty.

Procedures

- Read each frame in the left-hand column, while covering the right-hand column with the mask provided.

- Write your response in the space provided. Experience has shown that if you don't write your response, you will not retain nearly as much information.

- Check your response by moving the mask so as to uncover the correct response in the right-hand column.

- If your response is correct, go to the next frame. Otherwise, study the frame again and try to understand why you were wrong.

- Some frames refer you to exhibits. These are in a separate booklet. Remove it and use it when you are asked to do so.

- At the end of each part there is a post test; you will find it in the separate booklet. When you have completed a part, complete the post test. If you have difficulty with it, review the frames on this topic.

- Do not skip frames. If you have difficulty with a particular point, go back to the frame in which it was first mentioned and review it from there.

- NOTE: Halfway through the book, the pages reverse so that the response column will always be on the right-hand side of the page.

Technical Conventions

_____ = Fill in the one word that is missing.

.... = Fill in the one or more words that are missing.

__ __ __ __ __ = Fill in the letters that are missing, one to each underline.

. . . [Yes / No] = Underline or circle the correct alternative.

INSTRUCTOR'S GUIDE

An Instructor's Guide containing an overview of the text, instructions on how to use *Essentials of Accounting*, and quiz and examination material is provided free to instructors upon adoption of the text.

The Instructor's Guide may be obtained by contacting your local sales representative, or by calling Prentice Hall's Customer Service at 1-800-922-0579

Part 1

Basic Concepts

Learning Objectives

In this part you will learn:

- The nature of the balance sheet.
- The accounting meaning of assets, liabilities, and equity.
- The first five of the nine concepts that govern all accounting:
    - The dual-aspect concept.
    - The money-measurement concept.
    - The entity concept.
    - The going-concern concept.
    - The asset-measurement concept.
- The meaning of the principal items reported on a balance sheet.

1-1. Accounting is a language. The purpose of any language is to convey information. Accounting information is provided by reports called **financial statements.** This program helps you understand what the numbers in the financial statements mean and how they can be used. Please tear out Exhibit 1 (in the separate booklet) to see one of these financial statements. As indicated by the title at the top of the page, this report is called a _ _ _ _ _ _ _ sheet.

| Balance |

> *On an item like this, fill in one letter for each underline and then compare it with the correct answer, found here.*

> **NOTE:** Be sure to cover up the answers with the mask provided.

CONCLUDING NOTE

You now know the essentials of accounting. There is, of course, much more to the subject. Nonetheless, you now have a basic framework into which you can fit many other transactions when you encounter them. Moreover, notes are added to the financial statements which help explain them and give more detail than the statements themselves. You should always read these notes carefully.

We have used a common set of terms throughout this program. Unfortunately, there is no standard set of terms. Companies can use other terminology. Nonetheless, from your knowledge of the nature of the balance sheet and the income statement, you can usually figure out what is meant by a term that is not used in this program.

Some transactions are governed by specific rules that are not descried in this introductory treatment. For further study, see *Accounting: Text and Cases,* Tenth Edition, Robert N. Anthony, David F. Hawkins, and Kenneth A. Merchant (Irwin McGraw-Hill, 1999).

ACKNOWLEDGMENTS

Dr. Matthew Israel developed the program for the first edition.
Dr. Philip E. Meyer, Boston University, developed the original glossary.
Cameron E. H. Breitner contributed in a significant way to Part 8.
Betty Cloud was Professor Anthony's efficient, hard-working, cheerful secretary.
John C. S. Breitner was exceptionally patient and helpful during the revision process.
Darrianne P. Christian made useful comments for the 8th Edition.
We appreciate the advice and help of all these persons.

ELEMENTS OF THE BALANCE SHEET

1-2. A balance sheet gives financial information about an **entity.** The name of the entity that this balance sheet refers to is __ __ __ __ __ __ __ __ __ __ __ __ __ __ .

Garsden
Company

1-3. An entity is any organization for which financial statements are prepared. A business is an __ __ __ __ __ __ __ ; a college, a government, a church, and a synagogue are also __ __ __ __ __ __ __ __ __ .

entity
entities

1-4. The balance sheet is a snapshot of the financial position of the entity as of one moment in time. As indicated by the heading in Exhibit 1, the balance sheet for Garsden Company reports its financial position as of December 31, __ __ __ __ .

2002

1-5. The date December 31, 2002, means [circle A or B]:

    A. it was prepared on December 31, 2002.

    B. it reports the entity's financial position as of December 31, 2002.

B
(*Probably, it was prepared early in 2003.*)

1-6. The Garsden Company balance sheet has two sides. The heading of the left side is A __ __ __ __ __ __ , and the heading of the right side is L __ __ __ __ __ __ __ __ __ __ __ and E __ __ __ __ __ __ . We shall describe the meaning of each side.

Assets
Liabilities   Equity

ASSETS

1-7. Assets are valuable resources owned by the entity. An entity needs cash, equipment, and other resources in order to operate. These resources are its a __ __ __ __ __ __ . The balance sheet shows the amounts of each of these assets as of a certain date.

assets

- The interpretation of ratios is different in nonprofit organizations. Ratios will have meaning only to the extent that both their numerator and denominator are appropriate measurements.

- Nonprofit organizations often have goals that are nonfinancial in nature. We must choose appropriate performance measures to complement the information provided in their financial statements.

You have completed Part 11 of this program. If you think you understand the material in this part, you should now take Post Test 11, which is in the separate booklet. If you are uncertain about your understanding, you should review Part 11.

The post test will serve both to test your comprehension and to review the highlights of Part 11. After taking the post test, you may find that you are unsure about certain points. You should review these points.

1-8. Assets are resources **owned** by Garsden Company. Its employees, although usually its most valuable resource, . . . [are / are not] accounting assets.

> **NOTE:** On an item like this, circle the answer of your choice.

are not
(*No one owns humans since the abolition of slavery.*)

LIABILITIES AND EQUITY

1-9. The right side of the balance sheet shows the sources of funds that provided the entity's assets. As the heading indicates, there are two general types of sources, L _ _ _ _ _ _ _ _ _ _ _ and E _ _ _ _ _ .

Liabilities
Equity

1-10. **Liabilities** are the entity's obligations to outside parties who have furnished resources. These parties are generally called **creditors** because they have extended credit to the entity. As Exhibit 1 indicates, suppliers have extended credit in the amount of $5,602,000 as indicated by the item A _ _ _ _ _ _ _ p _ _ _ _ _ _ .

Accounts payable

1-11. Creditors have a **claim** against the assets in the amount shown as the liability. For example, a bank has loaned funds to Garsden Company, and therefore has a current claim of $1,000,000 of this amount, as indicated by the item, _ _ _ _ _ _ _ _ _ _ _ _ _ _ _ _ _ .

Bank loan payable

1-12. Because an entity will use its assets to pay its claims, the claims are claims against _ _ _ _ _ _ _ . They are claims against all the assets, not any particular asset.

assets

11-62. You also learned about the amount of capital tied up in inventory by looking at the inventory turnover ratio. Many nonprofit organizations do not use i _____ in the way that for-profits use it. Often the inventory in nonprofits is a supplies inventory rather than a sales inventory. This makes the i _____ t _____ ratio potentially meaningless for performance measurement, too.

inventory

inventory turnover

11-63. A ratio is the relationship between the numerator and the denominator. Before measuring performance by using a r _____, we must ask if both the n __ __ __ __ __ __ __ __ __ and the d __ __ __ __ __ __ __ __ __ __ __ have meaning for the analysis we are trying to do. If the answer is no, then another type of p _____ m _____ may be better.

ratio

numerator

denominator

performance measure

11-64. The financial statements tell only a part of the story about an entity. Since nonprofits have goals that are often nonfinancial in nature, [we can use the same analysis as a for-profit uses / we must develop other measures of performance].

we must develop other measures of performance

KEY POINTS TO REMEMBER

- Some entities have no ownership; we refer to such organizations as nonprofit or not-for-profit organizations.

- Nonprofit organizations have three financial statements, just as for-profit businesses have: the statement of financial position, the statement of activities, and the statement of cash flows.

- Net assets is the portion of the statement of financial position occupied by equity on a balance sheet. The three categories of net assets are unrestricted, temporarily restricted, and permanently restricted.

- Revenues from contributions must be classified as unrestricted, temporarily restricted, or permanently restricted. Revenues from services provided are unrestricted revenues.

- Both realized and unrealized gains on investments are reported as unrestricted revenues.

- Transfers from temporarily restricted funds occur when the funds are used for their specified purpose.

1-13. The other source of the funds that an entity uses to acquire its assets is called **Equity.** In Garsden Company, equity investors provided funds for which they received common stock. The total amount supplied by equity investors is called **Total paid-in capital.** In Garsden Company, it was $___ ___ , ___ ___ ___ ,000. (We shall describe the details in a later part.)

$12,256,000

> **NOTE:** The term is "Equity" (singular) not "Equities" (plural) even though there are several sources of equity.

1-14. Equity funds also come from a second source, the profits or **earnings** generated by the entity. The amount of these earnings that has not been paid to equity investors in the form of dividends is retained in the entity, and therefore is called __ __ __ __ __ __ __ __ earnings. In Garsden Company, the amount was $___ ___ , ___ ___ ___ ,000.

Retained
$13,640,000

1-15. Creditors can sue the entity if the amounts due them are not paid. Equity investors have only a *residual claim;* if the entity is dissolved, they get whatever is left after the liabilities have been paid, which may be nothing. Liabilities therefore are a . . . [stronger / weaker] claim against the assets, and equity is a . . . [stronger / weaker] claim.

stronger
weaker

DUAL-ASPECT CONCEPT

1-16. Whatever assets remain after the liabilities are taken into account will be claimed by the equity investors. Consider the case of an entity whose assets total $10,000, and whose liabilities total $4,000. Its equity must be $_____.

$6,000 (= $10,000 – $4,000)

> *A single blank indicates that the answer is one word or, when preceded by the dollar sign as it is here, one amount.*

1-17. (1) Any assets not claimed by creditors will be claimed by equity investors, and (2) the total amount of claims (liabilities + equity) cannot exceed what there is to be claimed. Therefore, the total amount of assets will always be . . . [greater than / equal to / less than] the total amount of liabilities plus equity.

equal to

11-57. In Exhibit 15 find the amount of the transfer from temporarily restricted net assets to unrestricted net assets. The total amount of transfers is $_____, and the net effect of the transfers is [plus $7,370 / minus $7,370 / $0].

$7,370 $0

11-58. Use the exhibit to show that revenues for the period 2002 increase net assets and expenses decrease net assets. The beginning amount of unrestricted net assets for 2002 is $_____. The total of unrestricted revenues for 2002 is $_____, and the total of unrestricted expenses is $_____. The surplus, or c _____ in n _____ a _____, is $_____. If you add the beginning net assets to the change in net assets, you arrive at the ending unrestricted net assets figure of $_____.

$51,835
$21,804
$16,025   change
net assets $5,779

$57,614

SIMILARITIES

11-59. The financial statements of nonprofit organizations are similar to those of for-profit companies in almost as many ways as they are different. For example, nonprofit organizations are **required** to recognize the c _____ of using up long-lived tangible assets. However, d _____ need not be recognized for certain works of art and historical treasures.

cost   depreciation

11-60. Nonprofit organizatons must prepare a statement of cash flows to accompany the statement of f _____ p _____ and the statement of a _____. This statement of cash flows looks very similar to the ones you learned about in Part 9.

financial position
activities

LIMITATIONS OF RATIO ANALYSIS

11-61. In Part 10 you learned to use some tools to measure financial performance. **Equity** investors invest in a business to earn a profit. Non _____ organizations do not have equity investors, so the return on e _____ is [still the best overall measure of performance / somewhat meaningless] for these entities. This does not mean that we should ignore the surplus, or the difference between revenues and expenses.

nonprofit
equity   somewhat meaningless

1-18. Here is the balance sheet of Garsden Company, greatly condensed so as to focus on the main elements, and disregarding the thousands:

GARSDEN COMPANY
Balance Sheet as of December 31, 2002
(000 omitted)

Assets		Liabilities & Equity	
Cash	$ 1,449	Liabilities	$12,343
Other assets	36,790	Equity	25,896
Total	$38,239	Total	$38,239

The total of the left side is $__ __ , __ __ __ ,000, and the total of the right side is $__ __ , __ __ __ ,000.

$38,239,000
$38,239,000

1-19. This is another way of saying that total assets must always equal total __ __ __ __ __ __ __ __ __ __ plus __ __ __ __ __ __ .

liabilities   equity

1-20. The fact that total assets must equal, or **balance,** total liabilities plus equity is why the statement is called a __ __ __ __ __ __ __ __ __ __ __ __ __ . This equality tells nothing about the entity's financial condition; it always exists unless the accountant has made a mistake.

balance
sheet

1-21. This equality leads to what is called the **dual-aspect concept.** The two aspects to which this concept refers are (1) _____ and (2) _____ plus _____, and the concept states that these two aspects are always _____. (In what relation to each other?)

assets
liabilities   equity
equal

1-22. The dual-aspect concept is the first of nine fundamental accounting concepts we shall describe in this program. The concept can be written as an equation, that is, a statement that something is equal to something else. Write this equation, using the words Assets, Liabilities, and Equity:

_____ = _____ + _____

Assets = Liabilities + Equity

11-51. To be certain you understand how the transfer process works, re-call the closing process from Part 3. In Part 3 (see Frame 3-62) you learned that [balance sheet / income statement] accounts are temporary accounts and [balance sheet / income statement] accounts are permanent accounts. This will help you to understand how t _____ s work.

income statement

balance sheet

transfers

11-52. You also learned that ultimately revenues [increase / decrease] the equivalent of equity and that expenses [increase / decrease] the equivalent of equity. This, too, will help you to understand how transfers work.

increase

decrease

11-53. Complete the journal entry for a contribution of $5,000 to a non-profit in 2002 for a program to take place in 2003.

Dr. Cash (temporarily restricted) $5,000

Cr. R _____ s (temporarily restricted) $5,000

Revenues

11-54. Now provide the journal entry to close the temporarily restricted revenue account to net assets at the end of 2002.

Dr. R _____ s (temporarily restricted) .... $_____

Cr. N _____ A _____ (temporarily restricted) $_____

Revenues $5,000

Net assets $5,000

11-55. In 2003 when the program takes place, the journal entry would be:

Dr. _____ _____ (_____ _____) $_____

Cr. R _____ s (unrestricted) $_____

Net assets (temporarily restricted) $5,000

Revenues $5,000

11-56. At the end of 2003, the un _____ revenues account will close to un _____ n _____ a _____.

unrestricted

unrestricted net assets

1-23. Suppose a business had assets totaling $20,000 and liabilities totaling $18,000. Evidently, its equity was $_____.

$2,000 = ($20,000 − $18,000)

Always equal!

The two sides **balance.**

1-24. At the close of business on December 31, 2001, Dowling Company had $2,000 in its bank account. It owned other assets totaling $24,000. The company owed $10,000 to creditors. Its equity was $16,000. Complete the balance sheet for Dowling Company:

DOWLING COMPANY

Balance Sheet as of _____

Assets		Liabilities and Equity	
Cash	$	Liabilities	$
Other assets		Equity	
Total	$	Total	$

December 31, 2001

$ 2,000	$10,000
24,000	16,000
$26,000	$26,000

1-25. If Dowling Company prepared a balance sheet as of the beginning of business the next day, January 1, 2002, would it be different from the one you prepared above? . . . [Yes / No]

No (*because nothing changes between the close of business on one day and the beginning of business on the next day*)

1-26. The term "Net assets" is sometimes used instead of "equity." It refers to the fact that equity is always the difference between A _____ and L _____. (We shall describe the details in a later part.)

Assets

Liabilities

> **NOTE:** You will see the term "Net Assets" instead of "Equity" on some balance sheets.

11-45. If the financial statements for Mercer Community Services are typical for nonprofits like Mercer, it is [customary that fees from services make up the majority of unrestricted revenues / customary that alternative sources of revenue make up the majority of unrestricted revenues / too difficult to tell from the information provided.]

customary that alternative sources of revenue make up the majority of unrestricted revenues *(If the statements are typical, this would be the case.)*

TRANSFERS

11-46. As you learned earlier, sometimes contributions from donors are recorded in the category of t _____ ly restricted. This means that there is a designated **purpose** for the contribution specified by the d _ _ _ _ _ .

temporarily

donor

11-47. Funds must remain in the temporarily restricted category of n _ _ a _ _ _ _ _ s until the accounting period when they are used for their designated p _ _ _ _ _ _ _ .

net assets
purpose

11-48. As restricted funds are used for their designated purpose, they must be transferred from their holding pattern to the unrestricted category on the statement of activities. This t _ _ _ _ _ _ _ _ of funds allows the reader to see that the entity has used funds held for a specific purpose.

transfer

11-49. Current operating activities of a nonprofit entity are found in the unrestricted revenues and expenses on the s _____ of a _____ s. Therefore, contributions for activities that are to take place in the future will not be recorded in the unrestricted portion of the statement of activities. Rather, they will stay in the category of temporarily restricted n _ _ a _ _ _ _ _ s until such time as they are used.

statement
activities

net assets

11-50. Although the total amount of net assets will not change as a result of a transfer, the individual categories will change. Evidently the sum total of all t _ _ _ _ _ _ _ _ s is zero.

transfers

MONEY-MEASUREMENT CONCEPT

1-27. If a fruit store owned $200 in cash, 100 dozen oranges, and 200 apples, could you add up its total assets from this information? . . . [Yes / No]

No (*because you can't add apples and oranges*)

Cash	$200
	100 dozen
	200
	————
	Can't add

1-28. To add together objects as different as apples, oranges, automobiles, shoes, cash, supplies, etc., they must be stated in . . . [different / similar] units.

similar

1-29. Can you add the amounts of apples and oranges if they are stated in terms of money? . . . [Yes / No]

Yes (*You could also add them to get "pieces of fruit," but this is not a useful number for accounting purposes.*)

1-30. The facts that appear in an accounting report are stated in units of money; that is, dollars and cents. This is the **money-measurement concept.** By converting different facts to monetary amounts, we can deal with them . . . [verbally / arithmetically]; that is, we can add one item to another, or we can _____ one item from another.

arithmetically
subtract

1-31. The money-measurement concept states that accounting reports only those facts that can be stated as m __ __ __ __ __ __ __ a __ __ __ __ __ __ .

monetary
amounts

1-32. If facts cannot be expressed in monetary terms, they cannot be reported on a balance sheet. Which of the following facts could be learned by reading a balance sheet of Able Company?

    A. How much cash Able Company has.

    B. The health of the president of Able Company.

    C. How much money Able Company owes.

    D. A strike is beginning at Able Company.

    E. How many automobiles Able Company owns.

A and C
(*Not E because the number of automobiles is not a monetary amount.*)

11-39. Sometimes the organization does not sell stocks or bonds that have increased in value but decides to hold them for the future. At the end of each accounting period, the organization must determine the market value of these investments, too. Although the gain, if there is one, is not immediately available unless the stock is sold, it must be reported as revenue. This unr _____ ed gain is just as much a part of revenues on the statement of unrestricted activities as d __ __ __ __ __ __ __ __ s and i __ __ __ __ __ __ t or other realized g _____ s.

unrealized
dividends
interest   gains

11-40. The financial statements for Mercer Community Services in Exhibit 15 are typical of those for a nonprofit organization. Evidently Mercer had investments that provided income and realized and un _____ ed gains.

unrealized

11-41. Also, evidently there were restrictions on some of the investment i __ __ __ __ __ __ . The income on Mercer's long-term investments was [unrestricted / temporarily restricted / permanently restricted / some of each].

income
some of each

11-42. Mercer apparently had both unr _____ ed and realized g _____ s on its long-term investments. In Exhibit 15, the total net realized and unrealized gains on all categories of long-term investments is $_____ .

unrealized
gains

$7,900,000

11-43. From Exhibit 15, the total amount of revenue that Mercer received from fees from its services was $_____ . This is _____% of the total unrestricted revenues for the period ending June 30, 2002.

$2,700,000
12.4%

11-44. Unrestricted revenues from contributions amounted to _____% of the total unrestricted revenues for the period ending June 30, 2002.

19.8%

1-33. Because accounting reports include only facts that can be stated in monetary amounts, accounting is necessarily a(n) . . . [complete / incomplete] record of the status of a business and . . . [does / does not] always give the most important facts about a business.

incomplete

does not

ENTITY CONCEPT

1-34. Accounts are kept for **entities,** rather than for the persons who own, operate, or otherwise are associated with those entities. For example, suppose Green Company is a business entity, and Sue Smith is its owner. Sue Smith withdraws $100 from the business. In preparing financial accounts for Green Company, we should record the effect of this withdrawal on the accounts of . . . [Sue Smith / the entity].

the entity

The accounting entity

Owner

NOT the
accounting entity

1-35. Sue Smith withdraws $100 from Green Company, of which she is the sole owner. Smith now has $100 more cash, but she has $100 less equity in Green Company. Smith is . . . [better off / worse off / no better or worse off] than she was before.

no better or worse off

1-36. [If Smith withdraws $100 from Green Company, of which she is the sole owner, she is just as well off after this withdrawal as before.] What about Green Company? It now has . . . [$100 more / the same amount / $100 less] in assets.

$100 less

1-37. The fact that accounts are kept for entities as distinguished from the persons associated with those entities is called the e __ __ __ __ __ concept.

entity

11-34. This means that in addition to revenues from operating activities and from contributions, revenues from i _ _ _ _ _ _ _ _ _ _ s will also appear as increases in unrestricted net assets. This can make the interpretation of the financial statements of a nonprofit very challenging.

investments

11-35. The investment portion of an organizations's assets derived from donations is called an endowment. An endowment can earn a return for the organization in several different ways. Funds invested in bonds or put into a bank earn i _ _ _ _ _ _ _ t. Interest income is a source of revenue.

interest

11-36. Unless the use of interest earned is restricted, it will be reported as r _____ in the statement of un _____ed activities.

revenue   unrestricted

11-37. Funds may also be invested in stocks of private entitites. Recall from earlier parts that some companies pay dividends to shareholders. Although a nonprofit organization does not have s _____ s or owners, it can own stock in another company as an investment. D _____ s earned from stock investments will also be reported as revenues in the statement of un _____ ed activities, according to accounting regulations.

shareholders

Dividends
unrestricted

11-38. Investments may be made in stocks that don't pay d _ _ _ _ _ _ _ s or in bonds that don't pay i _ _ _ _ _ _ _ t. Investors hope that such investments will result in higher stock or bond prices at some time in the future. If the entity sells its stock or bond investments for more than the original cost, there is a realized gain at the time of the sale.

dividends   interest

1-38. Owners of some small retail stores (called "mom and pop" stores) may not identify the cost of merchandise they withdraw for personal use, personal telephone calls, and the like. If this is so, then they do not apply the _ _ _ _ _ _ concept. Consequently, the financial statements of these stores are inaccurate.

entity

> **NOTE:** A business may be organized under any one of several legal forms: a corporation, a partnership (two or more owners), or a proprietorship (a single owner). The entity concept applies regardless of the legal status.

1-39. John and Ellen own the John and Ellen Laundry, a partnership. Each takes $1,000 cash from the partnership entity and deposits it into a personal bank account. An accounting report of the financial position of the John and Ellen Laundry would show that:

   A. the change in the entity's equity is zero.

   B. the entity has $2,000 less cash.

   C. the entity has $2,000 less equity.

   D. John and Ellen each have $1,000 more cash.

B and C
(*John's and Ellen's personal statements would show that each had $1,000 more cash.*)

> **NOTE:** Municipalities, hospitals, religious organizations, colleges, and other nonprofit or nonbusiness organizations are also accounting entities. Although in this program we focus primarily on businesses, the accounting for nonprofit entities is similar. (We will describe accounting for nonprofit entities later.)

GOING-CONCERN CONCEPT

1-40. Every year some entities go bankrupt or cease to operate. Most entities, however, keep on going from one year to the next. Accounting must assume either that (a) entities are about to cease operations, or (b) they are likely to keep on going. The more realistic assumption for most entities is . . . [(a) / (b)].

(b)

1-41. Accounting assumes that an entity, or **concern,** normally will keep on **going** from one year to the next. This assumption is therefore called the g _ _ _ _ _ - **concern concept.**

going

11-29. If a donor imposes a r _ _ _ _ _ _ _ _ _ _ _ n on a contribution, the revenue from that contribtution will ultimately increase
t _____ r _____ed net assets or p _____
r _____ed net assets.

restriction

temporarily restricted   permanently
restricted

11-30. Since revenues from services provided and revenues from contributions can both be considered un _____, both types of revenues will appear together on a statement of unrestricted activities.

unrestricted

> **NOTE:** The classification of revenues and expenses within the three cate-
> gories of net assets does not preclude the organization from incorporating
> additional classifications or explanations within a statement of activities. For
> example, within a category of net assets, the nonprofit organization may dis-
> tinguish between operating and nonoperating items.

11-31. Some contributions do not qualify as revenues. For example, contributions of works of art, historical treasures, and similar assets need not
be recognized as r _____ s if the donated items are added to
collections held for public exhibition, education, or research to further
public service rather than financial gain.

revenues

11-32. Apparently, the accounting for many transactions for nonprofit
organizations [is straightforward and easy / is more complex than for-
profit accounting].

is more complex than for-profit
accounting

11-33. Some nonprofits have funds invested in a way that will provide
dividend, interest, or noncash returns. According to accounting regulations for nonprofit organizations, the gains and losses on such investments must be reported as increases or d _____ in unrestricted
net assets unless their use is temporarily or permanently restricted by the
donor or by the law.

decreases

1-42. Specifically, the g _ _ _ _ _ - c _ _ _ _ _ _ _ concept states that accounting assumes that an entity will continue to operate indefinitely unless there is evidence to the contrary.

going-concern

> **NOTE:** If the entity is not a going concern, special accounting rules apply; they are not discussed in this introductory program.

1-43. Because of the going-concern concept, accounting . . . [does / does not] report what the assets could be sold for if the entity ceases to exist.

does not

> **NOTE:** We next describe the concepts that govern the measurement of asset amounts on the balance sheet. Most monetary assets are reported at their *fair value,* and most nonmonetary assets are reported at an amount that is based on their *cost.* These concepts, and the reasoning behind them, are introduced in this section.

ASSET-MEASUREMENT CONCEPT

1-44. Readers of the balance sheet want to know what the reported assets are worth. In accounting, the name for what an asset is "worth" is its *fair value* (also called *market value*). The Garsden Company balance sheet (Exhibit 1) reported that the company's cash on December 31, 2002, was $1,449,000. This was the f _ _ _ _ v _ _ _ _ _ of the asset Cash. We can be reasonably certain that the amount was actually $1,449,000 because the banks in which cash was deposited have reliable records of the amount.

fair value

1-45. Also, we can be reasonably certain that the _ _ _ _ _ _ _ _ _ _ _ of marketable securities was $246,000 because a stock exchange publishes a reliable record of the value as of December 31, 2002, for each security that it trades.

fair
value

1-46. In general, an asset is reported at its fair value when reliable information as to its market value is available. Usually, this information is obtained from an outside party. Thus, the concept is: **If reliable information is available, an asset is measured as its** _ _ _ _ _ _ _ _ _ _ .

fair
value

11-24. The classification of net assets is thus either r _____ or u _____, depending on the intentions of the d __ __ __ __ .

restricted
unrestricted   donor

> **NOTE:** It is important to understand the intentions of donors because they affect how organizations can subsequently use funds. There are more complications with respect to the classification of net assets that go beyond the scope of this introductory text.

REVENUES, EXPENSES, AND INVESTMENTS

11-25. Revenues are realized for nonprofits in much the same way as they are in for-profit organizations. Remember the r _____ concept, which states that r __ __ __ __ __ __ __ is recognized when goods and services are [paid for / delivered]. So when a nonprofit organization provides services, it recognizes the revenue associated with the service provided.

realization
revenue
delivered

11-26. The distinction between a revenue and an inflow of c __ __ __ is treated much the same way as it would be in a for-profit entity. If services are provided in 2002 but are not paid until 2003, the revenue is recognized in [2002 / 2003] in keeping with the realization concept. When this happens, the account called a _____ r _____ is debited in 2002 with the accompanying credit to sales revenue.

cash

2002
accounts receivable

11-27. Revenues from contributions are different from revenues earned on services provided. Recall that all revenues ultimately increase net assets (similar to their role in increasing equity in a for-profit). In a nonprofit, revenues are considered i _____ in unrestricted n _____ a _____ unless the use of the assets received is limited.

increases
net assets

11-28. Similarly, expenses are considered d _____ in unrestricted net assets.

decreases

1-47. The fair value of most assets is known on the date the asset was acquired because the buyer and the seller agreed on the amount. If Garsden Company purchased a plot of land in 1992 for $100,000, this land would have been reported on its December 31, 1992, balance sheet as $100,000. What was its fair value on December 31, 2002?

    A. $100,000

    B. More than $100,000

    C. Garsden doesn't know.

C
(Because the fair value may have changed for any number of good reasons.)

1-48. Because it doesn't know the fair value of the land on December 31, 2002, Garsden would report the amount at $100,000, which was its _ _ _ _ _ .

cost

1-49. If on December 31, 2002, Garsden owned machinery that it had purchased five years earlier for $50,000 with an estimated life of 10 years, it would probably report the asset amount as . . . [$50,000 / less than $50,000] representing the amount of cost that has not yet been used up. (Calculating this amount involves depreciation, described in Part 7.)

less than $50,000

1-50. In general, land, buildings, equipment, and inventories have this characteristic; their f _ _ _ _ v _ _ _ _ _ cannot be reliably measured except at the time they were acquired. They are reported at _ _ _ _ _ or a number based on cost.

fair value

cost

1-51. The asset-measurement concept combines both types of assets illustrated above. It is: **If reliable information is available, the amount of an asset is measured at its _ _ _ _ _ _ _ _ _ _ _ . Otherwise the measurement is based on its _ _ _ _ _ .**

fair value

cost

11-18. Assets can be donated for specific uses in a designated accounting period. Once used for the special purpose for which they were intended, they are no longer available. These assets are called t _ _ _ _ _ _ _ _ ly restricted assets.

temporarily

11-19. U _ _ _ _ _ _ _ _ _ _ _ ed net assets are those that result from profitable operating activities or from donations with no r _____ s.

Unrestricted

restrictions

11-20. There are many examples of assets in each of the three categories. If a donor gave land to an organization to use as part of ongoing operations, this donation would fit into the category of [permanently restricted / temporarily restricted / unrestricted] net assets because the purpose of the donation would be for the permanent future operations of the organization.

permanently restricted

11-21. Likewise, the donation of works of art to a museum would be considered permanently restricted n _____ a _____ .

net assets

11-22. The donation of funds for a specific program to take place in May 2003, however, would fit into the category of [permanently restricted / temporarily restricted / unrestricted] net assets because the funds [would continue to be available indefinitely / would be used up after the program ended]. Until May 2003, however, the funds could not be used for other purposes.

temporarily restricted

would be used up after the program ended

11-23. If you receive a phone call from someone asking you to donate funds to your college and you agree to do so, those funds would probably fit into the category of [permanently restricted / temporarily restricted / unrestricted] net assets. Unless you specify that your donation is to be saved for a specific purpose, or saved indefinitely and invested for a monetary return, it would show on the statement of financial position as u _____ n _____ a _____ .

unrestricted

unrestricted net assets

1-52. There are two reasons for measuring some assets at cost. First, estimating fair value of each asset may be expensive and unreliable. If you bought a pair of shoes for $100 in 2001 and asked two friends in 2002 for the shoes' value, they probably would disagree. Even if the estimates were made by professionals, the appraised value of each asset in a company would be . . . [subjective / objective] and . . . [expensive / inexpensive].

subjective *(that is, influenced by personal feelings rather than facts)*
expensive

1-53. Second, many assets are not going to be sold in the near future; they will be used in ongoing operations. The entity and those who use its balance sheet therefore . . . [do / do not] need to know the fair value of these assets. This reason stems from the previous concept, the g _ _ _ _ _ - c _ _ _ _ _ _ _ concept.

do not

going-concern

1-54. To summarize, the two reasons that accounting focuses on costs, rather than on fair values for some assets, are:

1. fair values are difficult to estimate; that is, they are . . . [objective / subjective], whereas costs are . . . [objective / subjective], and

2. the _ _ _ _ _ _ - _ _ _ _ _ _ _ _ concept makes it unnecessary to know the market value of many assets; the assets will be used in future operations rather than being sold immediately.

subjective
objective
going-concern

1-55. The decision of whether an asset is accounted for at fair value or at cost is usually made at the time the asset is acquired. For example, if a shoe retailer purchased an inventory of shoes for $1,000, they would be accounted for at (or recorded at) $1,000, which was their _ _ _ _ _ . If the retailer expected to sell the shoes for at least $1,500, they would be reported on the balance sheet at . . . [$1,000 / $1,500 / somewhere between $1,000 and $1,500].

cost

$1,000
(Any higher amount is a subjective opinion.)

11-13. Nonprofit organizations are [the same as / very different from] for-profits with respect to their purpose or m _ _ _ _ _ _ n. If we seek to measure their performance using only the monetary amounts, we would neglect important aspects of their missions and goals. Therefore, the f _____ s _____ limit the information we have for performance measurement to those aspects that can be expressed in m _ _ _ _ _ _ _ _ amounts.

very different from
mission

financial statements

monetary

11-14. Some of a nonprofit's g _ _ _ _ s can be measured by using financial statement information. For nonprofits, however, the surplus is not always an appropriate m _____. Performance measures need to be tied to goals and therefore [are the same / are likely to be different] for nonprofit organizations.

goals

measure
are likely to be different

NET ASSETS

11-15. One important difference in a balance sheet or statement of financial position of a nonprofit is the term n _ _ assets. This term represents the portion of the statement that is occupied by e _____ in a for-profit organization.

net
equity

11-16. Three types of net assets must be reported on a statement of financial position. The types are distinguished according to the level of restriction imposed on them by donors. The three types are:

1. permanently r _ _ _ _ _ _ _ ed net assets
2. temporarily restricted n _____ a _____
3. unr _ _ _ _ _ _ _ _ ed net assets

restricted
net assets
unrestricted

11-17. Some assets are donated to nonprofit organizations for specific purposes. Some are donated for holding rather than selling. Other assets with similar restrictions are to be invested to provide a permanent source of income to the organization. All such assets fit into the category of p _ _ _ _ _ _ _ _ ly restricted assets.

permanently

1-56. Monetary assets are those that have a claim on a specified amount of money. Cash, securities, and bonds mentioned above are . . . [monetary / nonmonetary] assets. Land, buildings, equipment, and inventory are . . . [monetary / nonmonetary] assets. In general, but with some exceptions described in later parts, **monetary assets are reported at fair value; nonmonetary assets are reported at cost or an amount based on cost.**

monetary

nonmonetary

1-57. Accounting does not report what many of the individual assets are worth, that is, their f __ __ __ v __ __ __ __ . Accounting therefore . . . [does / does not] report what the whole entity is worth. Those who criticize accounting for its failure to report an entity's "worth" do not appreciate that to do so would be difficult, subjective, and unnecessary.

fair value
does not

REVIEW OF ACCOUNTING CONCEPTS

1-58. The asset-measurement concept is the fifth of the nine fundamental accounting concepts. The first five are:

1. dual-aspect concept
2. money-measurement concept
3. entity concept
4. going-concern concept
5. asset-measurement concept

The dual-aspect concept is:

__ __ __ __ __ __ =

__ __ __ __ __ __ __ __ __ __ __ + __ __ __ __ __ __ .

Assets =
Liabilities + Equity

The money-measurement concept is:
Accounting reports only facts that can be expressed in m __ __ __ __ __ __ __ a __ __ __ __ __ __ __ .

monetary amounts

The entity concept is:
Accounts are kept for e __ __ __ __ __ __ __ __ as distinguished from the p __ __ __ __ __ __ __ who own those entities.

entities

persons

11-8. Nonprofit entities also have three basic financial statements. The status report for a nonprofit is similar to the [income statement / balance sheet] and is called a s _ _ _ _ _ _ _ _ _ t of financial position. The flow report is similar to the [income statement/balance sheet] and is called a statement of activities. The third statement, called a s _ _ _ _ _ _ _ _ _ t of c _ _ _ _ _ _ f _ _ _ _ _ _ s, has the same name in a nonprofit entity.

balance sheet

statement

income statement

statement   cash flows

11-9. Just like the b _ _ _ _ _ _ s _ _ _ _ _ _, the statement of financial position reports amounts for the organization's a _ _ _ _ _ _, l _ _ _ _ _ _ _ _ _ _ _, and equivalent of e _ _ _ _ _. Since there is no equity or ownership in a nonprofit, this last term is the **net difference** between the assets and the liabilities and is called n _ _ a _ _ _ _ _ _.

balance sheet

assets   liabilities
equity

net assets

11-10. In a for-profit entity, the operating **expenses** (or activities) portrayed on the income statement cause equity to increase or decrease. Similarly, in a nonprofit, the change in net assets is reflected in its statement of a _ _ _ _ _ _ _ _ _ s.

activities

11-11. Finally, a nonprofit reports the change in its **cash** and cash equivalents in a [balance sheet / income statement / statement of cash flows.]

statement of cash flows

DIFFERENT MISSIONS AND GOALS

11-12. A primary goal of a for-profit enterprise is to earn a p _ _ _ _ _ _ _. Therefore, the financial statement that measures this best is the [balance sheet / income statement / statement of cash flows.] You learned earlier that a good analysis must incorporate information from [the income statement alone / the balance sheet and the income statement / all three financial statements] because all of the financial statements together provide information on different aspects of financial performance.

profit
income statement

all three financial statements

The going-concern concept is:

Accounting assumes that an e __ __ __ __ __ __ will continue to operate

i __ __ __ __ __ __ __ __ __ __ __ __ .

entity
indefinitely

The asset-measurement concept is:

Accounting focuses on the __ __ __ __ __   __ __ __ __ __ of monetary

assets and on the __ __ __ __ __ of nonmonetary assets.

fair value
cost

BALANCE SHEET ITEMS

1-59. Refer to Exhibit 1 in your booklet. This is the balance sheet we introduced in Part 1. It reports the amounts of a __ __ __ __ __ __ ,

l __ __ __ __ __ __ __ __ __ __ __ , and e __ __ __ __ __ __ of Garsden

Company as of _____ .

assets
liabilities   equity
December 31, 2002

1-60. Remember that the note "($000 omitted)" means that the numbers are reported in thousands of dollars. For example, the number reported for Cash, $1,449, means that the amount of cash was $_____ . This is common practice. It is done to make the numbers easier to read; users are not interested in the details of the last three digits.

$1,449,000

1-61. Recall also that the total of the assets always equals the total of the liabilities plus equity. Total assets were $_____ , and total liabilities plus equity were $_____ .

$38,239,000
$38,239,000

1-62. Most items on a balance sheet are summaries of more detailed accounts. For example, the cash is probably located in a number of separate bank accounts, in cash registers, and in petty cash boxes. The total of all the cash is $_____ , rounded to the nearest thousand dollars.

$1,449,000 (*NOT $1,449*)

> **NOTE:** In the remainder of this part, we explain the meaning of some of the items on this balance sheet. Those not described here will be explained in later parts.

11-3. Some examples of organizations with no **ownership** are museums, hospitals, colleges and universities, private schools, research organizations, churches and synagogues, cultural organizations, foundations, social service organizations, and advocacy groups. Although these organizations may be very different from one another, they all share one common trait. They do not have shareholders or o _ _ _ _ _ s.

owners

11-4. Nonprofit organizations are also exempt from paying taxes in most states. The regulations to determine nonprofit status may differ from state to state. To quality as a n _ _ _ _ _ _ _ _ _ t organization, application must be made to the governing body in the state in which the organization resides.

nonprofit

11-5. In Part 2 you learned that the terms "profit," "earnings," "surplus," and "income" all have the same meaning. They refer to the **excess** of r _ _ _ _ _ _ _ s less e _ _ _ _ _ _ _ s. Nonprofit organizations can have the equivalent of profitable operations however. To simplify, for nonprofit entitites we often just use the term "surplus," or e _ _ _ _ _ _ of revenues less expenses.

revenues   expenses

excess

11-6. Remember that the Equity section of the balance sheet reports the amount of capital that the for-profit entity has obtained from two different sources:

1. The amount paid in by the owner(s), which is called P _____ - _____ C _____.

Paid-
in Capital

2. The amount of income that has been retained in the entity, which is called R _____ E _____.

Retained Earnings

11-7. Since no dividends are paid in nonprofit organizations, the retained earnings are equal to the accumulated s _ _ _ _ _ _ _ _ s. Some nonprofit organizations do receive contributions from persons outside the entity. They are not called **paid-in capital** but are indeed sources of c _____.

surpluses

capital

NOTE: Please refer back to Exhibit 1 in your booklet. It is the Balance Sheet for Garsden Company. In this next part, we explain the meaning of some of the items on this balance sheet. Those not described here will be explained in later parts.

ASSETS

1-63. Assets as val __ __ __ __ __ res __ __ __ __ __ __. Let's make this idea more specific. In order to count as an asset in accounting, an item must pass three tests.

valuable resources

1-64. The first requirement is that the item must be **controlled** by the entity. Usually this means that the entity must **own** the item. If Able Company rents a building owned by Baker Company, this building . . . [is / is not] an asset of Able Company. The building . . . [is / is not] an asset of Baker Company.

is not

is

NOTE: Certain leased items, called capital leases, are assets and are an exception to this rule. They are described in Part 7.

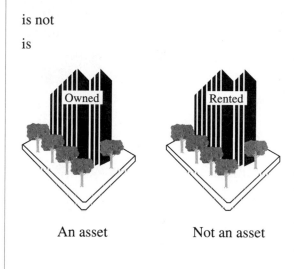

An asset   Not an asset

1-65. In accounting, the employees of an entity are not assets because the entity does not _____ them. However, if a baseball club owns a contract in which a player agrees to provide his services, the contract . . . [is / is not] an asset.

own

is (*The asset is the contract, not the player, and it is an asset only if it passes the third test, in Frame 1-67.*)

1-66. The second requirement is that the item must be **valuable** to the entity. Which of these would qualify as assets of a company that sells dresses?

A. The company's right to collect amounts owed by customers.

B. Regular dresses held for sale.

C. Dresses that no one wants because they have gone out of style.

D. A cash register in working condition.

E. A cash register that doesn't work and can't be repaired.

A, B, and D

Part 11

Nonprofit Financial Statements

Learning Objectives

In this part, you will learn:

- The nature of nonprofit or not-for-profit organizations.
- How financial statements of nonprofit organizations are different.
- How equity differs from net assets.
- Why ratio analysis for nonprofits may be different.

NONPROFIT ORGANIZATIONS

11-1. In earlier parts you learned that when revenues are greater than expenses, the result of such **profitable** operations is net i __ __ __ __ __   income

or p __ __ __ __ . You learned also that the equity section of the balance   profit

sheet reports the amount of capital that the entity has obtained from its

shareholders or o __ __ __ __ s, as well as the income that has been re-   owners

tained in the account called _____ _____ .   retained earnings

11-2. Some entities have no ownership. Such entitites do not obtain cap-

ital from shareholders and do not pay d _____ . These entities   dividends

are called nonprofit or not-for-p __ __ __ __ __ organizations. For our   profit

purposes both of these terms have the same meaning.

1-67. The third requirement is that the item must have been acquired at a **measurable cost.** Jones Company bought a trademark from another company for $1 million; this trademark . . . [is / is not] an asset of Jones Company.

is

1-68. By contrast, if Jones Company has built up an excellent reputation because of the consistently high quality of its products, this reputation . . . [is / is not] an asset in accounting, even though it may be worth many millions of dollars.

is not

1-69. To summarize, for an item to be listed as an asset, it must meet three requirements:

1. It must be __ __ __ ed or c __ __ __ __ __ __ __ __ __ ed by the entity;

owned   controlled

2. It must be v __ __ __ __ __ __ __ __ to the entity; and

valuable

3. It must have been acquired at a m __ __ __ __ __ __ __ __ __ __

measurable

c __ __ __ .

cost

> **NOTE:** Assets are divided into two main categories—current and noncurrent—and liabilities also are divided into these categories. They are introduced in the following section and explained in more detail in Part 2.

1-70. Current assets are cash and other assets that are expected to be converted into cash or used up in the near future, usually within one year. Groceries on the shelves of a grocery store . . . [are / are not] current assets. The store build-

are

ing . . . [is / is not] a c __ __ __ __ __ __ __ __ a __ __ __ __ __ . On the balance

is not   current asset

sheet, current assets are usually reported separately from noncurrent assets. They are expected to be converted to cash within a year.

> PLEASE DON'T PEEK: If you look at the answer before writing your response, you will lose much of the educational value.

1-71. Current assets consist of c _____ and of assets that are

cash

expected to be converted into c _____ or used up within a short

cash

period, usually within _____ _____ (how long?).

one year

1-72. As the name suggests, assets that are expected to be useful for longer than one future year are called . . . [current / noncurrent] assets.

noncurrent

KEY POINTS TO REMEMBER

- The financial statements do not tell the whole story about an entity because they report only past events, do not report market values, and are based on judgments and estimates. Nevertheless, they provide important information.

- Financial statements are analyzed by using ratios, rather than absolute dollar amounts. These ratios are compared with those for the same entity in the past, with those for similar entities, or with standards based on judgment.

- An overall measure of performance is Return on Equity (ROE). It takes into account both profitability and the capital used in generating profits. Another overall measure is Return on Permanent Capital, or Return on Investment, which is the ratio of profits (adjusted for interest and taxes) to total permanent capital.

- An entity with a low profit margin can provide a good return on equity investment if it has a sufficiently high capital turnover.

- In addition to information about profitability, financial statements provide information about the entity's liquidity and solvency.

You have completed Part 10 of this program. If you think you understand the material in this part, you should now take Post Test 10, which is in the separate booklet. If you are uncertain about your understanding, you should review Part 10.

The post test will serve both to test your comprehension and to review the highlights of Part 10. After taking the post test, you may find that you are unsure about certain points. You should review these points before going on to Part 11.

LIABILITIES

1-73. The right-hand side of the Garsden Company balance sheet lists the company's liabilities and equity. As explained in Part 1, these can be regarded either as c _ _ _ _ _ against the assets or as the s _ _ _ _ _ _ from which the assets were acquired. The claims of creditors and other outside parties are called l _ _ _ _ _ _ _ _ _ _ .

claims

sources

liabilities

1-74. In Exhibit 1, the first category of liabilities is _____ liabilities. As you might expect from the discussion of current assets, current liabilities are claims that become due within a . . . [short / long] time, usually within _____ _____ (how long?).

current

short
one year

1-75. As we have seen, Garsden Company has obtained funds by borrowing, and $_____ of this debt is not due to be repaid until after December 31, _____. This amount is therefore a . . . [current / noncurrent] liability.

$2,000,000
2003
noncurrent

1-76. Liabilities are claims against all the assets. The $5,602,000 of accounts payable on the Garsden Company balance sheet is a claim against . . . [the current assets of $22,651,000 / the total assets of $38,239,000].

the total assets of $38,239,000

CURRENT RATIO

1-77. The current assets and current liabilities indicate the entity's ability to meet its current obligations. A measure of this ability is the **current ratio,** which is the ratio of **current** assets to **current** liabilities. For Garsden Company, the current ratio is:

$$\frac{\$22,651,000}{\$\ 9,519,000} = 2.4 \text{ to } 1$$

---
* Carry this amount to one decimal place.

10-70. The return on permanent capital is the same in both companies, as you can see for yourself in the following calculation.

	EBIT margin	* Capital turnover	= Return on permanent capital	
Supermarket	0._____	* _____ times =	____ %	0.04 * 10 = 40%
Department store	0._____	* _____ times =	____ %	0.20 * 2 = 40%

TESTS OF FINANCIAL CONDITION

> **NOTE:** A business must be concerned with more than profitability. It must also maintain a sound financial condition. This means that it must be able to pay its debts when they come due.

10-71. Ability to meet current obligations is called **liquidity.** The ratio of current assets to current liabilities, called the _____ ratio, is a widely used measure of liquidity.

current

10-72. Solvency measures the entity's ability to meet its obligations when they come due. If a high proportion of permanent capital is obtained from debt, rather than from equity, this increases the danger of insolvency. The proportion of debt is indicated by the d __ __ __ r __ __ __ __ .

debt ratio

> **NOTE:** Any of dozens of other ratios may be used for various purposes in analyzing the profitability and financial condition of a business. Those described here are the ones in most general use. Others give a more detailed picture of the important relationships.

10-73. Financial analysts form their opinions about a company partly by studying ratios such as those we have presented. They also study the details of the financial statements, including the notes that accompany these statements. They obtain additional information by conversations and visits because they realize that the financial statements tell . . . [only part of the / the whole] story about the company.

only part of the

1-78. In Garsden's industry, a current ratio of at least 2 to 1 is desirable. Garsden Company . . . [does / does not] pass this test.

does

EQUITY

1-79. Equity consists of capital obtained from sources that are not liabilities. As Exhibit 1 indicates, there are two sources of equity capital: (1) $12,256,000, which is labeled Total _____ - _____ _____ and (2) $13,640,000, which is labeled _____ _____.

Paid-in

Capital   Retained

Earnings

1-80. Paid-in Capital is the amount of capital supplied by equity investors. They own the entity. The details of how this item is reported depends on the type of organization. Garsden Company is a corporation, and its owners receive *shares* of common _____ as evidence of their ownership. They are therefore called s __ __ __ __ holders. Other forms of ownership will be described in Part 8.

stock

share (or stockholders)

1-81. The Paid-in Capital is reported as two separate amounts: $1,000,000, which is labeled _____ _____, and $11,256,000, labeled Additional _____ - _____ _____. The reasons for this distinction are described in Part 8. The important number is the total amount paid in by the shareholders, which is $_____.

Common Stock

Paid-in Capital

$12,256,000

1-82. Individual shareholders may sell their stock to someone else, but this has no effect on the balance sheet of the corporation. The market price of shares of General Motors Corporation stock changes almost every day; the amount of Paid-in Capital reported on the General Motors balance sheet . . . [does / does not] reflect these changes. This is consistent with the e _____ concept; transactions between individual shareholders do not affect the entity.

does not

entity

1-83. The other equity item, $13,640,000, shows the amount of equity that has been *earned* by the profitable operations of the company and that has been *retained* in the entity; hence the name, R __ __ __ __ __ __ __ E __ __ __ __ __ __ __ .

Retained

Earnings

10-68. For example, consider the following results for a supermarket and a department store, each with $10 million of sales revenue.

	Supermarket	Department store
	(000 omitted)	
Sales revenue	$10,000	$10,000
EBIT	400	2,000
Permanent capital	1,000	5,000

The EBIT margin for the supermarket is only

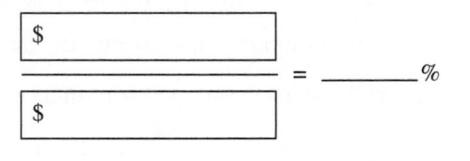 = _____%

$$\frac{\$400}{\$10,000} = 4\%$$

and for the department store it is

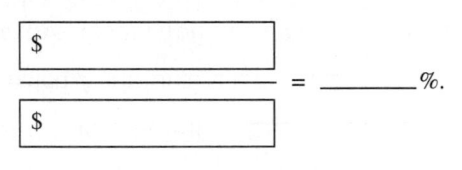 = _____%.

$$\frac{\$2,000}{\$10,000} = 20\%$$

The ratio for the department store is much . . . [lower / higher].

higher

10-69. However, the department store has more expensive fixtures, a larger inventory, and a lower inventory turnover than the supermarket, so its capital turnover is lower. Calculate the capital turnover of each.

	Sales	÷ Permanent Capital	= Capital turnover
Supermarket	$_____	÷ $_____	= _____ times
Department store	$_____	÷ $_____	= _____ times

$10,000 ÷ $1,000 = 10 times

$10,000 ÷ $5,000 = 2 times

1-84. Retained Earnings represents those amounts that have been retained in the entity after part of the company's earnings (i.e., profits) have been paid to shareholders in the form of dividends. Complete the following equation:

Retained Earnings = – _____ .

Earnings – Dividends

1-85. Retained Earnings are additions to equity that have accumulated since the entity began, not those of a single year. Therefore, unless Garsden Company has been in business only one year, the $13,640,000 shown as Retained Earnings as of December 31, 2002, reflects . . . [one / all previous] year(s) of operations.

all previous

1-86. The amount of Retained Earnings shows the amount of capital generated by operating activities. It is **not** cash. Cash is an asset. On December 31, 2002, the amount of Cash was $_____. The amount of Retained Earnings was $_____.

$1,449,000
$13,640,000

1-87. Always keep in mind the fundamental accounting equation:

 = _____ + _____ .

Assets = Liabilities + Equity

The right-hand side of the balance sheet shows the *sources* of capital. The capital itself exists in the form of __ __ __ __ __ __ , which are reported on the left-hand side.

assets

KEY POINTS TO REMEMBER

• The assets of an entity are the things of value that it owns.

• The sources of funds used to acquire assets are:

    1. liabilities and
    2. equity.

• Liabilities are sources from creditors.

10-64. Another way of finding the return on permanent capital is to multiply the EBIT margin ratio by the capital turnover. Calculate this relationship.

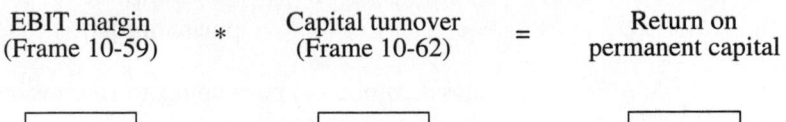

EBIT margin (Frame 10-59)	*	Capital turnover (Frame 10-62)	=	Return on permanent capital
☐ %	*	☐	=	☐ %

14% * 1.8 = 25%

10-65. This formula suggests two fundamental ways in which the profitability of a business can be improved:

1. . . . [Increase / Decrease] the EBIT margin ratio.

    Increase

2. . . . [Increase / Decrease] the capital turnover.

    Increase
    (*If you had difficulty in following these relationships, try some numbers of your own.*)

COMMENTS ON PROFITABILITY MEASUREMENT

10-66. In the analysis above, we used ratios because absolute dollar amounts are . . . [rarely / often] useful in understanding what has happened in a business.

rarely

10-67. Also, we focused on *both* income and the capital used in earning that income. Focusing on just one of these elements can be . . . [just as good / misleading].

misleading

- Equity consists of (1) funds obtained from equity investors, who are owners, and (2) retained earnings, which result from the entity's profitable operation.

- Creditors have a strong claim on the assets. They can sue if the amounts due them are not paid. Equity investors have only a residual claim.

- Total assets equal the total of liabilities plus equity. This is the dual-aspect concept.

- The amounts of assets, liabilities, and equity as of one point in time are reported on the entity's balance sheet.

- Accounting reports only those facts that can be stated in monetary amounts. This is the money-measurement concept.

- Business accounts are kept for entities, rather than for the persons who own, operate, or otherwise are associated with those entities. This is the entity concept.

- Accounting assumes that an entity will continue to operate indefinitely. This is the going-concern concept.

- Monetary assets are reported at their fair value; other assets are reported at a number based on cost. This is the asset-measurement concept.

- Assets arc valuable items that are owned or controlled by the entity and that were acquired at a measurable cost. Goodwill is not an asset unless it was purchased.

- Current assets arc cash and other assets that are expected to be converted into cash or used up in the near future, usually within one year.

- Current liabilities are obligations due in the near future, usually within one year.

- The current ratio is the ratio of current assets to current liabilities.

- Equity consists of paid-in capital (which in a corporation is represented by shares of stock) plus earnings retained since the entity began. It does not report the market value of the stock. Retained earnings is not cash; it is part of the owners' claim on the assets.

You have completed Part 1 of this program. If you think you understand the material in this part, you should now take Post Test 1, which is in the separate booklet. If you are uncertain about your understanding, you should review Part 1.

The post test will serve both to test your comprehension and to review the highlights of Part 1. After taking the post test, you may find that you are unsure about certain points. You should review these points before going on to Part 2.

10-60. The permanent capital as of December 31, 2002, is the debt capital (i.e., noncurrent liabilities) of $_____,000 plus the equity capital of $_____,000, a total of $_____,000. The return on permanent capital is found by dividing EBIT by this total. Calculate the return on permanent capital.

$$\frac{\rule{3cm}{0.4pt}}{\rule{2cm}{0.4pt} \quad \rule{1cm}{0.4pt}} = \frac{\$\rule{2cm}{0.4pt}}{\$\rule{2cm}{0.4pt}} = \boxed{\quad} \%$$

$40
$130 $170(= $40 + $130)

$$\frac{\text{EBIT}}{\text{Permanent capital}} = \frac{\$42}{\$170} = 25\%$$

10-61. Copy the numerator and denominator of the return on permanent capital on Line 4 of Exhibit 14.

Numerator: EBIT (Earnings before interest and taxes)
Denominator: Permanent capital

10-62. Another ratio shows how much sales revenue was generated by each dollar of permanent capital. This ratio is called the **capital turnover** ratio. Calculate it for Arlen Company.

$$\text{Capital turnover} = \frac{\text{Sales revenue}}{\text{Permanent capital}} = \frac{\$\rule{2cm}{0.4pt}}{\$\rule{2cm}{0.4pt}} = \boxed{\quad} \text{ times}$$

$$\frac{\$300}{\$170} = 1.8 \text{ times}$$

Copy the numerator and denominator of this ratio on Line 13 of Exhibit 14.

Numerator: Sales revenue
Denominator: Permanent capital

10-63. American manufacturing companies have a capital turnover ratio of roughly two times on average. A company that has a large capital investment in relation to its sales revenue is called a **capital-intensive** company. A capital-intensive company, such as a steel manufacturing company or a public utility, has a relatively . . . [high / low] capital turnover.

Part 2

Balance Sheet Changes; Income Measurement

Learning Objectives

In this part you will learn:

- The meaning of the principal items reported on a balance sheet.
- How several types of transactions change the amounts reported on the balance sheet.
- The nature of income and the income statement.

> **NOTE:** Assets are divided into two main categories—current and noncurrent—and liabilities also are divided into these categories. They are explained in the following section.

CURRENT ASSETS

2-1. Current assets are cash and other assets that are expected to be converted into cash or used up in the near future, usually within ___ ___ ___ ___ ___ ___.

one

year

2-2. Securities are stocks and bonds. They give valuable rights to the entity that owns them. The U.S. Treasury promises to pay stated amounts of money to entities that own treasury bonds. Therefore, U.S. Treasury Bonds owned by Garsden Company . . . [are / are not] assets of Garsden Company.

are

10-56. We have focused on return on equity (ROE) as an overall measure of performance. Another useful measure is the **return on permanent capital.** This shows how well the entity used its capital, without considering how much of its permanent capital came from each of the two sources: d __ __ __ and e __ __ __ __ __ . This ratio is also called **return on investment (ROI).**

debt   equity

10-57. The *return* portion of this ratio is *not* net income. Net income includes a deduction for interest expense, but interest expense is the return on debt capital. Therefore, net income . . . [understates / overstates] the return earned on all permanent capital. Also, income tax expense is often disregarded to focus on pretax income.

understates

10-58. The return used in this calculation is **Earnings Before** the deduction of **Interest** and **Taxes** on income. It is abbreviated by the first letters of the words in boldface, or __ __ __ __ .

EBIT

10-59. As with other income statement numbers, Earnings Before Interest and Taxes (EBIT) is expressed as the percentage of sales revenue. This gives the **EBIT margin.** Calculate it for Arlen Company.

$\dfrac{\$42}{\$300} = 14\%$

Enter the numerator and denominator of the EBIT margin ratio on Line 7 of Exhibit 14.

Numerator: EBIT
Denominator: Sales revenue

2-3. Marketable securities are securities that are expected to be converted into cash within a year. An entity owns these securities so as to earn a return on funds that otherwise would be idle. Marketable Securities are . . . [current / noncurrent] assets.

current

> **NOTE:** Investments in safe, very short-term funds, such as money market funds, are often included in the cash item rather than in marketable securities. The item is then called cash and cash equivalents.

2-4. An **account receivable** is an amount that is owed to the business, usually by one of its customers, as a result of the ordinary extension of credit. A customer's monthly bill from the electric company would be an a __ __ __ __ __ __ r __ __ __ __ __ __ __ __ __ __ of the electric company until the customer paid the bill.

account receivable

2-5. Inventories are goods being held for sale, as well as supplies, raw materials, and partially finished products that will be sold upon completion. For example, a truck owned by an automobile dealer for resale to its customers . . . [is / is not] inventory. A truck owned by an entity and used to transport its own goods . . . [is / is not] inventory.

is

is not

2-6. In Exhibit 1 the inventories of Garsden Company are reported as $_____.

$10,623,000

2-7. An entity's burglar alarm system is valuable because it provides protection against loss. The burglar alarm system is an asset. Would a fire insurance policy that protects the entity against losses caused by fire damage also be an asset? . . . [Yes / No]

Yes

2-8. Entities buy fire insurance protection ahead of the period that the insurance policy covers. When they buy the insurance policy, they have acquired an a __ __ __ __ __ . Because the policy covers only a short period of time, the asset is a . . . [current / noncurrent] asset. Insurance protection can't be touched. It is an **intangible** asset.

asset

current

OTHER MEASURES OF PERFORMANCE

10-50. Another measure of performance is **earnings per share.** As the name suggests, the ratio is simply the total _____ for a given period, divided by the number of _____ of common stock outstanding.

earnings (*or* net income)

shares

10-51. Exhibit 10 shows that the earnings (i.e., net income) of Arlen Company in 2002 was $_____ and that the number of shares outstanding during 2002 was _____. Therefore, earnings per share was $_____.

$24,000

4,800

$5 (= $24,000 ÷ 4,800)

10-52. On line 2 of Exhibit 14 enter the numerator and denominator of the earnings-per-share ratio.

Numerator: Net income
Denominator: Number of shares outstanding

10-53. Earnings per share is used in calculating another ratio—the **price-earnings ratio.** It is obtained by dividing the average market price of the stock by the earnings per share. If the average market price for Arlen Company stock during 2002 was $35, then the price-earnings ratio is the ratio of $35 to $5, or _____ to 1.

7 (= $25 ÷ $5)

10-54. On line 3 of Exhibit 14, enter the numerator and denominator of the price-earnings ratio.

Numerator: Average market price
Denominator: Earnings per share

10-55. Price-earnings ratios of many companies are published daily in the financial pages of newspapers. Often, the ratio is roughly 9 to 1, but it varies greatly depending on market conditions. If investors think that earnings per share will increase, this ratio could be much higher—perhaps 15 to 1. Apparently, investors are willing to pay . . . [more / less] per dollar of earnings in a growing company.

more

2-9. Prepaid Expenses is the name for intangible assets that will be used up in the near future; that is, they are intangible . . . [current / non-current] assets. (The reason for using the word "expense" will be explained in Part 5.) Exhibit 1 shows that Garsden Company had $_____ of Prepaid Expenses on December 31, 2002.

current

$389,000

NONCURRENT ASSETS

2-10. Tangible assets are assets that can be touched; they have physical substance. Buildings, trucks, and machines are t __ __ __ __ __ __ __ assets. They are also . . . [current / noncurrent] assets.

tangible

noncurrent

2-11. As indicated by the first item listed under noncurrent assets in Exhibit 1, the usual name for tangible, noncurrent assets is _____, _____, and _____. Because they are noncurrent, we know that these assets are expected to be used in the entity for more than _____ _____ (how long?).

Property   Plant   Equipment

one year

2-12. Exhibit 1 shows the . . . [cost / market value] of property, plant, and equipment to be $26,946,000. It shows that a portion of the cost of this asset has been subtracted from the original cost because it has been "used up." This "used-up" portion is called _____ _____ and totals $_____.

cost

Accumulated
Depreciation $13,534,000

2-13. After this amount is subtracted, the asset amount is shown as $_____. This is the amount of cost that . . . [has / has not] been used up. (In Part 7, we shall explain this amount further.)

$13,412,000   has not

2-14. The other noncurrent asset items are **intangible assets**; that is, they have no physical substance, except as pieces of paper. The Investments item consists of securities, such as bonds. Evidently Garsden Company does not intend to turn these investments into cash within _____ _____ (how long?). If these securities were expected to be turned into cash within that period, they would be listed as a current asset, M __ __ __ __ __ __ __ __ __ __ S __ __ __ __ __ __ __ __ __ __ .

one

year

Marketable Securities

10-45. The final ratio we shall use in examining capitalization is the **debt ratio.** As explained in Part 8, this is the ratio of debt capital to total permanent capital. Noncurrent liabilities are d _____ capital, and noncurrent liabilities plus equity are t _____ p _____ capital. Calculate the debt ratio for Arlen Company.

debt
total
permanent

$$\frac{\boxed{}}{\boxed{} + } = \frac{\boxed{\$}}{\boxed{\$}} = \boxed{\%}$$

$$\frac{\text{Noncurrent liabilities}}{\text{Noncurrent liabilities} + \text{Equity}} = \frac{\$40}{\$40 + \$130} = 24\%$$

10-46. Copy the numerator and denominator of the debt ratio on Line 12 of Exhibit 14.

Numerator: Noncurrent liabilities
Denominator: Noncurrent liabilities + Equity

10-47. The larger the proportion of permanent capital that is obtained from debt, the smaller is the amount of equity capital that is needed. If Arlen had obtained $85,000 of its $170,000 permanent capital from debt, its debt ratio would have been _____%, and its ROE would have been . . . [higher / lower] than the 18.5% shown in Exhibit 13.

50%
higher

10-48. A high debt ratio results in a . . . [more / less] risky capital structure than does a low debt ratio.

more

10-49. In several of the calculations above, we used balance sheet amounts taken from the ending balance sheet. For some purposes, it is more informative to use an **average** of beginning and ending balance sheet amounts. Arlen Company had $130,000 of equity at the end of 2002. If it had $116,000 at the beginning of 2002, its *average* equity during 2002 was $_____. Since its net income in 2002 was $24,000, its return on *average* equity investment was _____%.*

$123,000
19.5% (= $24,000 ÷ $123,000)

---

* one decimal place.

2-15. The next noncurrent asset reported is **Patents and Trademarks.** These are rights to use patents and rights to valuable brand names or logos (such as "7 UP"). Because they are assets, we know that

1. they are v _ _ _ _ _ _ _ _ ,

2. they are o _ _ _ _ by Garsden Company, and

3. they were acquired at a measurable c _ _ _ .

valuable

owned

cost

2-16. Goodwill, the final item on the asset side, has a special meaning in accounting. It arises when one company buys another company and pays more than the value of its net identifiable assets. Grady Company bought Baker Company, paying $1,400,000 cash. Baker Company's identifiable assets were judged to be worth $1,500,000, and Grady became responsible for Baker's liabilities, which totaled $500,000. Complete the following calculation:

Baker's identifiable assets	$ _____	$1,500,000
less liabilities	_____	$500,000
Net identifiable assets	_____	$1,000,000
Grady paid Baker	$ 1,400,000	
Therefore, goodwill was	_____	$400,000

CURRENT LIABILITIES

2-17. In Exhibit 1, the first category of liabilities is _____ liabilities. As you might expect from the discussion of current assets, current liabilities are claims that become due within a . . . [short / long] time, usually within _____ _____ (how long?).

current

short

one year

2-18. The first current liability listed in Exhibit 1 is _____ _____. These are the opposite of Accounts Receivable; that is, they are amounts that . . . [the company owes to its suppliers / are owed to the company by its customers].

Accounts
Payable

the company owes to its suppliers

10-40. Calculate the current ratio for Arlen Company.

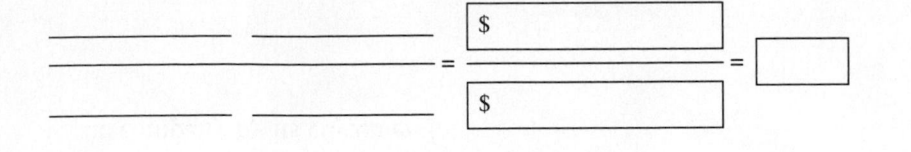

$$\frac{\text{Current assets}}{\text{Current liabilities}} = \frac{\$140}{\$60} = 2.3$$

10-41. Copy the numerator and the denominator of the current ratio on Line 10 of Exhibit 14.

Numerator: Current assets
Denominator: Current liabilities

10-42. If Arlen Company decreased its current ratio to 1.5 by increasing its current liabilities, this would . . . [increase / decrease] its ROE. However, such a low current ratio would . . . [increase / decrease] the possibility that Arlen would be unable to pay its current liabilities when they come due.

increase

increase

> **NOTE:** The numbers used here to calculate the current ratio are amounts as of the end of the year. Seasonal factors may greatly affect the current ratio during the year. For example, a department store may increase its inventory in the fall in anticipation of holiday business, and its current ratio therefore decreases. Similar limitations affect the other measures discussed in this part.

10-43. A variation of the current ratio is the **quick ratio** (also called the **acid-test ratio**). In this ratio, inventory is excluded from the current assets, and the remainder is divided by current liabilities. This is a more stringent measure of bill-paying ability than the current ratio. Calculate this ratio for Arlen Company:

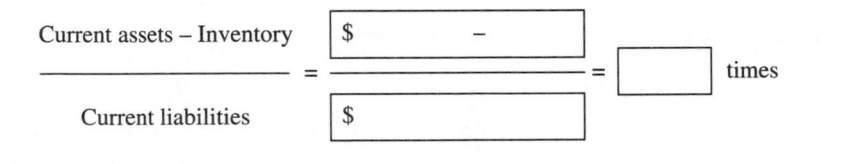

$$\frac{\$140 - \$60}{\$60} = 1.3$$

10-44. Copy the numerator and the denominator of the quick ratio on Line 11 of Exhibit 14.

Numerator: Current assets – Inventory
Denominator: Current liabilities

2-19. In December 2001, Smith Company sold a personal computer to Brown Company for $3,000. Brown Company agreed to pay for it within 60 days. On their December 31, 2001, balance sheets, Smith Company would report the $3,000 as Accounts . . . [Receivable / Payable] and Brown Company would report the $3,000 as Accounts . . . [Receivable / Payable].

Receivable

Payable

2-20. The next item, **Bank Loan Payable,** is reported separately from Accounts Payable because the debt is evidenced by a promissory n ___ ___ ___ . Which statement is true?

note

    A. Garsden owes the bank $1,000,000.

    B. Garsden will pay the bank $1,000,000.

    C. Both A and B are true.

A (*Although most liabilities will be paid, the balance sheet does not promise this.*)

> **NOTE:** Amounts owed to employees and others for services they have provided but for which they have not been paid are listed as **Accrued Liabilities.** They will be described in Part 5.

2-21. Estimated Tax Liability is the amount owed to the government for taxes. It is shown separately from other liabilities, both because the amount is large and also because the exact amount owed may not be known as of the date of the balance sheet. In Exhibit 1 this amount is shown as $_____. It is a current liability because the amount is due within _____ _____ (how long?).

$1,541,000

one year

2-22. Two items of **Long-term Debt** are shown as liabilities. One, labeled "current portion," amounts to $_____. The other, listed under noncurrent liabilities, amounts to $_____. Evidently, the total amount of long-term debt is $_____.

$500,000

$2,000,000

$2,500,000

2-23. The $500,000 is shown separately as a current liability because it is due within _____ _____ (how soon?), that is, before December 31, _____. The remaining $2,000,000 does not become due until after December 31, _____.

one year

2003

2003

10-36. The amount of capital tied up in inventory can be examined by calculating the **inventory turnover ratio.** Since inventory is recorded at cost, this ratio is calculated in relation to cost of sales, rather than to sales revenue.

Calculate the inventory turnover ratio for Arlen Company (refer to Exhibit 13 if necessary).

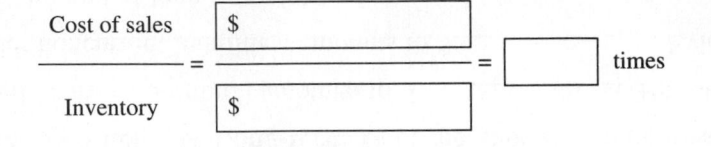

$$\frac{\text{Cost of sales}}{\text{Inventory}} = \frac{\$180}{\$60} = 3 \text{ times}$$

10-37. Copy the numerator and the denominator of the inventory turnover ratio on Line 9 of Exhibit 14.

Numerator: Cost of sales
Denominator: Inventory

10-38. If Arlen Company had maintained an inventory of $90,000 to support $180,000 cost of sales, its inventory turnover would have been _____ (how many?) times, rather than three times. With this change, its ROE would have been . . . [higher / lower] than the 18.5% shown in Exhibit 13.

two

lower

10-39. The **current ratio** is another way of examining the current section of the balance sheet. In an earlier part we pointed out that if the ratio of current assets to current liabilities is too low, the company might not be able to pay its bills. However, if the current ratio is too high, the company would not be taking advantage of the opportunity to finance current assets with current l _ _ _ _ _ _ _ _ _ _ s. Additional current liabilities would . . . [increase / decrease] its ROE. Equity inevitably would be lower; otherwise, the balance sheet would not balance.

liabilities

increase

NONCURRENT LIABILITIES

2-24. Suppose the $500,000 current portion was paid in 2003, and an additional $600,000 of debt became due in 2004. On the balance sheet as of December 31, 2003, the current portion of long-term debt would be reported as $_____, and the noncurrent liability would be reduced to $_____.

$600,000
$1,400,000

> **NOTE:** Although a single **liability** may have both a current portion and a noncurrent portion, a single asset is not always so divided. Prepaid Insurance of $2,000, covering protection for two future years, is usually reported as a current asset of $2,000.

> **NOTE:** The other noncurrent liability, Deferred Income Taxes, will be described in Part 7.

EQUITY

2-25. Recall that Equity consists of capital obtained from sources that are not liabilities. The two sources of equity capital for Garsden Company are Total _____ - ____ _____ and _____ _____.

Paid-in Capital
Retained Earnings

2-26. Recall also that the amount of equity that has been *earned* by the profitable operations of the company and that has been *retained* in the entity is called _____ _____.

Retained Earnings

BALANCE SHEET CHANGES

2-27. The amounts of assets, liabilities, and equity of an entity . . . [remain constant / change from day to day]. Therefore the amounts shown on its balance sheet also . . . [remain constant / change].

change from day to day
change

2-28. Although a balance sheet must be prepared at the end of each year, it can be prepared more often. In this part, you will be asked to prepare a balance sheet at the end of each day. We shall consider a business named Glendale Market, owned by a proprietor, John Smith. The **entity** here is . . . [John Smith / Glendale Market].

Glendale Market

10-31. If Camden Company could reduce its equity to $500,000, while still maintaining its net income of $60,000, its ROE would become _____%. Evidently, with net income held constant, Camden Company can increase its ROE by . . . [increasing / decreasing] its equity.

12% ($60,000 ÷ $500,000)

decreasing

10-32. Since total assets always equal liabilities plus equity, equity can be decreased only if (1) assets are . . . [increased / decreased], (2) liabilities are . . . [increased / decreased], or (3) there is some combination of these two types of changes.

decreased

increased

10-33. For example, Camden Company's equity would be decreased by $100,000 (to $500,000) if assets were decreased by $40,000 (to $960,000) and liabilities were . . . [increased / decreased] by $_____ (to $_____). If equity was $500,000 and net income was $60,000, ROE would be

increased

$60,000 $460,000

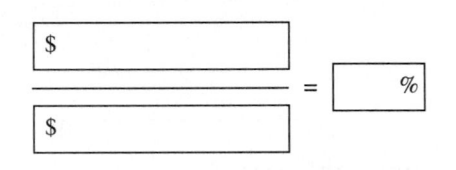

$$\frac{\$60,000}{\$500,000} = 12\%$$

10-34. In earlier parts, two ratios for measuring current assets were described. One related to accounts receivable and was called the **days' sales uncollected.** It shows how many days of sales revenue are tied up in accounts receivable.

Calculate days' sales uncollected for Arlen Company.

$$\frac{\text{Accounts receivable}}{\text{Sales revenue} \div 365} = \frac{\$}{\$ \div 365} = \boxed{} \text{ days' sales uncollected}$$

$$\frac{\text{Accounts receivable}}{\text{Sales revenue} \div 365} = \frac{\$40}{\$300 \div 365} = 49 \text{ days}$$

10-35. Copy the numerator and the denominator of the days' sales uncollected on Line 8 of Exhibit 14.

Numerator: Accounts receivable
Denominator: Sales revenue ÷ 365

2-29. On January 2, Smith started Glendale Market by opening a bank account in its name and depositing $10,000 of his money in it. In the assets column of the following balance sheet, enter the amount of Cash that Glendale Market owned at the close of business on January 2.

GLENDALE MARKET
Balance Sheet as of January 2

Assets	Liabilities & Equity
Cash . . . . $	

$10,000

2-30. Cash is money on hand and money in bank accounts that can be withdrawn at any time. On January 2, if John Smith deposited $8,500 in the bank instead of $10,000 and kept $1,500 in the cash register, its cash at the close of business on January 2 would be _____.

$10,000

2-31. Recall that a name for equity capital is "Paid-in Capital." In the space below, record the amount of paid-in capital as of the close of business on January 2.

GLENDALE MARKET
Balance Sheet as of January 2

Assets	Liabilities & Equity
Cash $10,000	. . $

Paid-in capital $10,000

2-32. This balance sheet tells us how much cash . . . [Glendale Market / John Smith] had on January 2. The separation of Glendale Market from John Smith, the person, is an illustration of the e _ _ _ _ _ _ concept.

Glendale Market

entity

> **NOTE:** An entity owned by one person, such as Glendale Market, is called a **proprietorship.** In some proprietorships, the equity item is labeled with the proprietor's name: "John Smith, Capital." This is simply a variation in terminology, not a difference in concepts.

10-26. The **profit margin percentage** is a useful number for analyzing net income. You calculated it in an earlier part. Calculate it for Arlen Company.

$$\frac{\text{Net income}}{\text{Sales revenue}} = \frac{\$24}{\$300} = 8\%$$

10-27. Copy the numerator and denominator of the profit margin percentage on Line 6 of Exhibit 14.

Numerator: Net income
Denominator: Sales revenue

10-28. Statistics on the average profit margin percentage in various industries are published and can be used by Arlen Company as a basis for comparison. Statistics on the average *dollar* amount of net income are not published. Such statistics . . . [are / are not] useful because sheer size is not a good indication of profitability.

are not

TESTS OF CAPITAL UTILIZATION

10-29. The bottom section of the diagram in Exhibit 13 shows the main components of Arlen Company's capital. The information is taken from its . . . [income statement / balance sheet]. We shall examine ratios useful in understanding these components.

balance sheet

10-30. As background for this analysis, let's examine some relationships in Camden Company, which has the following condensed balance sheet:

Assets	Liabilities and Equity	
	Total liabilities	$400,000
	Total equity	600,000
Total $1,000,000	Total	$1,000,000

If net income was $60,000, Camden Company's return on equity (ROE) was Net income ÷ Equity, or _____%.

10% (= $60,000 ÷ $600,000)

2-33. On January 2, Glendale Market received $10,000 cash from John Smith. To record the effect of this event on the financial condition of the entity, you made _____ (how many?) changes in the balance sheet. After you made these changes, the balance sheet . . . [did / did not] balance. This is an illustration of the d __ __ __ - a __ __ __ __ __ concept.

two

did

dual-aspect

2-34. A total should always be given for each side of the balance sheet. Complete the following balance sheet.

BROWN COMPANY
Balance Sheet as of June 30, 2001

Assets		Liabilities & Equity	
Cash	$50,000	Accounts payable	$10,000
		Paid-in capital	40,000
	$		$

Total $50,000   Total $50,000

2-35. The totals of the above balance sheet . . . [are equal by coincidence / are necessarily equal].

are necessarily equal

2-36. Amounts on a balance sheet are generally listed with the most current items first. Correct the following list to make it accord with this practice.

Liabilities (as of December 31, 2001):

Bank loan payable (due next October)

Accounts payable (due in 60 days)

Long-term debt

Accounts payable

Bank loan payable

Long-term debt

2-37. When an entity borrows money, it may sign a written promise to repay. Such a written promise is termed a **note.** For example, if Business A borrows money from Business B, signing a note, Business A will record a . . . [note receivable / note payable] on its balance sheet, and Business B will record a . . . [note receivable / note payable].

note payable

note receivable

10-22. One factor that affects net income is gross margin. In an earlier part, you calculated the **gross margin percentage.** Calculate it for Arlen Company.

$$\frac{\text{Gross margin}}{\text{Sales revenue}} = \frac{\$ *}{\$ } = \boxed{} \% \quad \text{gross margin}$$

$$\frac{\text{Gross margin}}{\text{Sales revenue}} = \frac{\$120}{\$300} = 40\%$$

> **NOTE**: If you have difficulty with this or other calculations, refer to Exhibit 13, where the amounts are calculated.

10-23. On Line 5 of Exhibit 14, write the name of the numerator and of the denominator of the gross margin percentage.

Numerator: Gross margin
Denominator: Sales revenue

10-24. Gross margin percentages vary widely. A profitable supermarket may have a gross margin of only 15%. Many manufacturing companies can have gross margins of about 35%. Compared with these numbers, the gross margin of Arlen Company is . . . [low / high].

high

> **NOTE**: Since companies even in the same industry can differ widely, it is often misleading to generalize about financial statistics.

10-25. A high gross margin does not necessarily lead to a high net income. Net income is what remains after expenses have been deducted from the gross margin, and the higher the expenses, the . . . [higher / lower] the net income.

lower

2-38. On January 3, Glendale Market borrowed $5,000 cash from a bank, giving a note therefor.

Change the following January 2 balance sheet so that it reports the financial condition on January 3. In making your changes, cross out any material to be changed and write the corrections like this:

15,000
~~10,000~~

GLENDALE MARKET
Balance Sheet as of January 2

Assets		Liabilities & Equity	
			.... $
Cash $10,000		Paid-in capital $10,000	
Total $10,000		Total $10,000	

GLENDALE MARKET 3
Balance Sheet as of January ~~2~~

Assets		Liabilities & Equity	
		Note payable $5,000	
Cash ...... 15,000 ~~$10,000~~		Paid-in capital $10,000	
Total ..... ~~$10,000~~ 15,000		Total .... ~~$10,000~~ 15,000	

2-39. To record the effect of the event of January 3, you made _____ (how many?) change(s) to the balance sheet (not counting the new totals and the new date) that were necessary. The change(s) ... [did / did not] affect the equality that had existed between assets and liabilities + equity.

two

did not

2-40. On January 4, Glendale Market purchased and received inventory costing $2,000, paying cash.

Change the following January 3 balance sheet so that it reports the financial condition on January 4. Strike out any items that must be changed, and write the corrections above (or below) them.

GLENDALE MARKET
Balance Sheet as of January 3

Assets		Liabilities & Equity	
Cash $15,000		Note payable .... $ 5,000	
....		Paid-in capital 10,000	
	....	Total $15,000	

GLENDALE MARKET 4
Balance Sheet as of January ~~3~~

Assets		Liabilities & Equity	
Cash ...... 13,000 ~~$15,000~~		Note payable .... $ 5,000	
Inventory $2,000		Paid-in capital 10,000	
Total $15,000		Total $15,000	

10-18. Arlen Company's net income in 2002 was $24,000. Baker Company's net income in 2002 was $50,000. From this information we cannot tell which company performed better. Why not?

Because we do not know Baker Company's equity.

10-19. Baker Company's equity was $1,000,000. Its net income in 2002 was $50,000. Its ROE was therefore

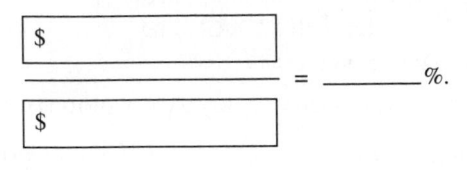

$$\frac{\$50,000}{\$1,000,000} = 5\%$$

Arlen Company with an ROE of 18.5% performed . . . [better / worse] than Baker Company.

better

10-20. The comparison of Arlen Company's dollar amount of net income with Baker's dollar amount . . . [did / did not] provide useful information. The comparison of their **ratios** or **percentage**s was . . . [useful / not useful]. Useful comparisons involve r _____ s or p _____ s.

did not

useful

ratios

percentages

FACTORS AFFECTING RETURN ON EQUITY

10-21. Ratios help explain the factors that influenced return on equity.

> **NOTE:** Some ratios were explained in earlier parts. We shall review these ratios and introduce others, using the financial statements of Arlen Company in Exhibit 10 and the diagram of these factors in Exhibit 13. These ratios are to be summarized in Exhibit 14.

We have already described the Return on Equity ratio, which is:

$$\frac{\text{(numerator) Net income}}{\text{(denominator) Equity}} = \text{Return on Equity}$$

Copy the numerator and denominator of this ratio on Line 1 of Exhibit 14.

Numerator: Net income
Denominator: Equity

2-41. The event of January 4 required two changes on the balance sheet, even though . . . [only one / both] side(s) of the balance sheet was (were) affected.

only one

2-42. Each event that is recorded in the accounting records is called a **transaction.** When Glendale Market received $10,000 from John Smith and deposited it in its bank account, this qualified as a _____ under the definition given above because it was "an event that was

transaction

__ __ __ __ __ __ __ __ in the __ __ __ __ __ __ __ __ __ __ __

recorded   accounting

__ __ __ __ __ __ __ ."

records

2-43. Each transaction you recorded has caused at least _____ (how many?) change(s) on the balance sheet (not counting the changes in the totals and in the date), even when only one side of the balance sheet was affected. This is true of all transactions, and this is why accounting is called a . . . [single / double / triple]-entry system.

two

double

2-44. Earlier we described the fundamental accounting equation, assets = liabilities + equity. If we were to record only *one* aspect of a transaction, this equation . . . [would / would not] continue to describe an equality.

would not

2-45. The fundamental accounting equation, which is _____ = _____ + _____ was also referred to in Part 1 as the d__ __ __ -aspect concept.

assets

liabilities   equity

dual

> **NOTE:** When a business sells merchandise for $300 that had cost it $200, the profit of $100 represents an increase of $100 in equity. As we saw in Part 1, the Retained Earnings item is used to record changes in equity arising from the operation of the business. These facts will help you in analyzing the transactions that follow.

10-13. In 2002, Arlen Company had net income of $24,000, and its equity on December 31, 2002, was $130,000. Calculate its ROE for 2002.

$$\frac{N \underline{\hspace{1cm}} \ i \underline{\hspace{2cm}}}{E \underline{\hspace{3cm}}} = \frac{\$ \boxed{}}{\$ \boxed{}} = \boxed{} \%^* \ \text{ROE}$$

$$\frac{\text{Net income}}{\text{Equity}} = \frac{\$24,000}{\$130,000} = 18.5\% \ \text{ROE}$$

_____

* one decimal place

10-14. In order to judge how well Arlen Company performed, its 18.5% ROE must be compared with something. If in 2001 Arlen Company had an ROE of 20%, we can say that its performance in 2002 was . . . [better / worse] than in 2001. This is the **historical** basis of comparison.

worse

10-15. If in 2002 another company had an ROE of 15%, Arlen's ROE was . . . [better / worse] than the other company's. Or if in 2002 the average ROE of companies in the same industry as Arlen was 15%, Arlen's ROE was . . . [better / worse] than the industry average. This is the **external** basis of comparison. If the other company is thought to be the best-managed company in the industry, this comparison is called **benchmarking.**

better

better

10-16. Finally, if from our experience we judge that a company like Arlen should have earned an ROE of 20% in 2002, we conclude that Arlen's ROE was . . . [better / worse] than this **judgmental standard.**

worse

10-17. Most comparisons are made in one or more of the three ways described above. Give the meaning of each.

1. **Historical:** comparing the entity with _____
   _____

   its own performance in the past

2. **External:** comparing the entity with _____
   _____

   another entity's performance or industry averages

3. **Judgmental:** comparing the entity with _____
   _____

   a standard based on our judgment

2-46. On January 5, Glendale Market sold merchandise for $300, receiving cash. The merchandise had cost $200.

Change the following January 4 balance sheet so that it reports the financial condition on January 5. (If you cannot do this frame, skip to the next without looking at the answer to this one.)

GLENDALE MARKET
Balance Sheet as of January 4

Assets		Liabilities & Equity	
Cash	$13,000	Note payable	$ 5,000
Inventory	2,000	Paid-in capital	10,000
		...	
Total	$15,000	Total	$15,000

$15,100 = $15,100

GLENDALE MARKET
Balance Sheet as of January ~~4~~ 5

Assets		Liabilities & Equity	
Cash	**13,300** ~~$13,000~~	Note payable	$ 5,000
Inventory	**1,800** ~~2,000~~	Paid-in capital	10,000
		Retained earnings	**100**
Total	~~$15,000~~ **15,100**	Total	~~$15,000~~ **15,100**

(If you answered this frame correctly, skip to Frame 2-53.)

2-47. On January 5, Glendale Market sold merchandise for $300 cash that cost $200.

To record this transaction, let's handle its individual parts separately. Change the date. Then, record only the amount of cash after the receipt of the $300. (Disregard, for the moment, any other changes, including changes in totals.)

GLENDALE MARKET
Balance Sheet as of January 4

Assets		Liabilities & Equity	
Cash	$13,000	Note payable	$ 5,000
Inventory	2,000	Paid-in capital	10,000
Total	$15,000	Total	$15,000

GLENDALE MARKET
Balance Sheet as of January ~~4~~ 5

Assets		Liabilities & Equity	
Cash	**13,300** ~~$13,000~~	Note payable	$ 5,000
Inventory	2,000	Paid-in capital	10,000
Total	$15,000	Total	$15,000

10-8. The opinion says that the auditors . . . [prepared / audited] the financial statements and that these statements are the responsibility of . . . [the auditors / management].

audited

management

10-9. The opinion further states that the financial statements . . . [accurately / fairly] present the financial results.

fairly
(Because judgments and estimates are involved, no one can say that the financial statements are entirely accurate.)

10-10. In the last paragraph of the opinion, the auditors assure the reader that the statements were prepared in conformity with g _____ a _____ a _____ p _____ .

generally

accepted accounting principles

> **NOTE:** Exhibit 12 is an example of a **clean** or **unqualified** opinion. If any of the above statements cannot be made, the auditors call attention to the exceptions in what is called a **qualified** opinion. A qualified opinion can be a serious matter. If the qualification is significant, securities exchanges can suspend trading in the company's stock.

OVERALL FINANCIAL MEASURES OF PERFORMANCE

> **NOTE:** Although they have **limitations,** financial statements usually are the most useful source of information about an entity. We shall focus first on what they tell about its overall **performance.**

10-11. Equity investors (i.e., shareholders) invest money in a business in order to earn a profit, or **return,** on that equity. Thus, from the viewpoint of the shareholders, the best overall measure of the entity's performance is the r _ _ _ _ _ _ that was earned *on* the entity's e _ _ _ _ _ _ . (This is abbreviated ROE.)

return   equity

10-12. The accounting name for the profit or return earned in a year is n _ _ i _ _ _ _ _ _ .

net income

Return on equity is the percentage obtained by dividing n _ _ i _ _ _ _ _ _ by e _ _ _ _ _ _ .

net

income   equity

2-48. On January 5, Glendale Market sold merchandise for $300 cash that cost $200. Merchandise that had cost $200 was removed from its inventory.

Record the amount of inventory after this transaction.

GLENDALE MARKET
Balance Sheet as of January ~~4~~ 5

Assets	13,300		Liabilities & Equity	
Cash	~~$13,000~~		Note payable	$ 5,000
Inventory	2,000		Paid-in capital	10,000
Total	$15,000		Total	$15,000

GLENDALE MARKET
Balance Sheet as of January ~~4~~ 5

Assets	13,300		Liabilities & Equity	
Cash	~~$13,000~~		Note payable	$ 5,000
Inventory	1,800 ~~2,000~~		Paid-in capital	10,000
Total	$15,000		Total	$15,000

2-49. On January 5, Glendale Market sold merchandise for $300 cash that cost $200.

Now total the assets as of the close of business on January 5, and show the new total.

GLENDALE MARKET
Balance Sheet as of January ~~4~~ 5

Assets	13,300		Liabilities & Equity	
Cash	~~$13,000~~		Note payable	$ 5,000
Inventory	1,800 ~~2,000~~		Paid-in capital	10,000
Total	$15,000		Total	$15,000

GLENDALE MARKET
Balance Sheet as of January ~~4~~ 5

Assets	13,300		Liabilities & Equity	
Cash	~~$13,000~~		Note payable	$ 5,000
Inventory	1,800 ~~2,000~~		Paid-in capital	10,000
Total	~~$15,000~~ 15,100		Total	$15,000

2-50. On January 5, Glendale Market sold merchandise for $300 cash that cost $200.

GLENDALE MARKET
Balance Sheet as of January ~~4~~ 5

Assets	13,300		Liabilities & Equity	
Cash	~~$13,000~~		Note payable	$ 5,000
Inventory	1,800 ~~2,000~~		Paid-in capital	10,000
Total	~~$15,000~~ 15,100		Total	$15,000

Evidently the transaction of January 5 caused a net . . . [decrease / increase] of $_____ in the assets of Glendale Market from what they had been at the close of business on January 4.

increase

$100

10-3. Third, the balance sheet does not show the . . . [cost / fair value] of nonmonetary assets. In accordance with the a _ _ _ _ _ - m _ _ _ _ _ _ _ _ _ _ _ concept, plant assets are reported at their . . . [unexpired cost / fair value].

fair value
asset
measurement
unexpired cost

Also, depreciation is a writeoff of . . . [cost / fair value]. It is *not* an indication of changes in the real value of plant assets. The balance sheet . . . [does / does not] show the entity's "net worth."

cost

does not

10-4. Fourth, the accountant and management have some latitude in choosing among alternative ways of recording an event in the accounts. An example of flexibility in accounting is that in determining inventory values and cost of sales, the entity may use the L _ _ _ , F _ _ _ , or average cost methods.

LIFO FIFO

10-5. Fifth, many accounting amounts are estimates. In calculating the depreciation expense of a plant asset, for example, one must estimate its s _ _ _ _ _ _ _ l _ _ _ _ and its r _ _ _ _ _ _ _ _ v _ _ _ _ .

service life residual
value

AUDITING

10-6. All large companies and many small ones have their accounting records examined by independent, certified public accountants. This process is called **auditing,** and the independent accountants are called _ _ _ _ _ tors.

auditors

10-7. After completing their examination, the _ _ _ _ _ _ _ _ _ s write a report giving their opinion. This o _ _ _ _ _ _ _ _ is reproduced in the company's annual report. A typical opinion is shown in Exhibit 12.

auditors
opinion

2-51. On January 5, Glendale Market sold merchandise for $300 that cost $200. The assets of the entity increased by $100. The increase was the result of selling merchandise at a profit. As we learned in Part 1, profitable operations result in an increase in equity, specifically in the item R _____ E _____ .

Retained Earnings

2-52. On January 5, Glendale Market sold merchandise for $300 that cost $200. Add $100 of Retained Earnings and show the new total of the right-hand side.

GLENDALE MARKET
Balance Sheet as of January ~~4~~ 5

Assets		Liabilities & Equity	
	13,300		
Cash	~~$13,000~~	Note payable	$ 5,000
	1,800		
Inventory	~~2,000~~	Paid-in capital	10,000
Total	~~$15,000~~ 15,100	Total	$15,000

GLENDALE MARKET
Balance Sheet as of January ~~4~~ 5

Assets		Liabilities & Equity	
	13,300	Note	
Cash	~~$13,000~~	payable	$ 5,000
	1,800	Paid-in	
Inventory	~~2,000~~	capital	10,000
		Retained earnings	100
Total	~~$15,000~~ 15,100	Total	~~$15,000~~ 15,100

2-53. On January 6, Glendale Market purchased merchandise for $2,000 and added it to its inventory. It agreed to pay the vendor within 30 days.

Change the following January 5 balance sheet so that it reports the financial condition on January 6. Recall that an obligation to pay a vendor is called an "Account Payable." Be sure to change the totals.

GLENDALE MARKET
Balance Sheet as of January 5

Assets		Liabilities & Equity	
Cash	$13,300		$
Inventory	1,800	Note payable	5,000
		Paid-in capital	10,000
		Retained earnings	100
Total	$15,100	Total	$15,100

GLENDALE MARKET
Balance Sheet as of January ~~5~~ 6

Assets		Liabilities & Equity	
Cash	$13,300	Accounts payable	$2,000
	3,800	Note	
Inventory	~~1,800~~	payable	5,000
		Paid-in capital	10,000
		Retained earnings	100
Total	~~$15,100~~ 17,100	Total	~~$15,100~~ 17,100

Part 10

Analysis of Financial Statements

Learning Objectives

In this part you will learn:

- The limitations of financial statement analysis.
- The nature and limitations of auditing.
- An approach to analyzing financial statements.
- Overall financial measures of performance.
- Other ratios used in financial statement analysis.

LIMITATIONS OF FINANCIAL STATEMENT ANALYSIS

> **NOTE:** In this part, we shall describe how information in financial statements is **used.** Before doing this, let's review the reasons that accounting cannot provide a **complete picture** of the status or performance of an entity.

10-1. One limitation is suggested by the word **financial;** that is, financial statements report only events that can be measured in m _ _ _ _ ary amounts.

monetary

10-2. A second limitation is that financial statements are historical; that is, they report only events that . . . [have happened / will happen], whereas we are also interested in estimating events that . . . [have happened / will happen]. The fact that an entity earned $1 million last year . . . [definitely predicts / is not necessarily an indication of] what it will earn next year.

have happened
will happen

is not necessarily an indication of

2-54. On January 7, merchandise costing $500 was sold for $800, which was received in cash.

Change the following January 6 balance sheet so that it reports the financial condition on January 7.

GLENDALE MARKET
Balance Sheet as of January 6

Assets		Liabilities & Equity	
Cash	$13,300	Accounts payable	$ 2,000
Inventory	3,800	Note payable	5,000
		Paid-in capital	10,000
		Retained earnings	100
Total	$17,100	Total	$17,100

GLENDALE MARKET
Balance Sheet as of January ~~8~~ 7

Assets		Liabilities & Equity	
Cash	**14,100** ~~$13,300~~	Accounts payable	$ 2,000
Inventory ..	**3,300** ~~3,800~~	Note payable	5,000
		Paid-in capital	10,000
		Retained earnings ...	**400** ~~100~~
Total	~~$17,100~~ **17,400**	Total	~~$17,100~~ **17,400**

2-55. On January 8, merchandise costing $600 was sold for $900. The customer agreed to pay $900 within 30 days. (Recall that when customers buy on credit, the entity has an asset called "Accounts Receivable.")

Change the following January 7 balance sheet so that it reports the financial condition on January 8.

GLENDALE MARKET
Balance Sheet as of January 7

Assets		Liabilities & Equity	
Cash	$14,100	Accounts payable	$ 2,000
	...	Note payable	5,000
Inventory	3,300	Paid-in capital	10,000
		Retained earnings	400
Total	$17,400	Total	$17,400

GLENDALE MARKET
Balance Sheet as of January ~~7~~ 8

Assets		Liabilities & Equity	
Cash	$14,100	Accounts payable	$ 2,000
Accounts receivable 900		Note payable	5,000
Inventory ..	**2,700** ~~3,300~~	Paid-in capital	10,000
		Retained earnings ...	**700** ~~400~~
Total	~~$17,400~~ **17,700**	Total	~~$17,400~~ **17,700**

- GAAP has specific requirements for determining which cash flows are classified as investing activities and which are classified as financing activities, but statement users need not memorize these rules because they are evident from the statement itself.

- When a company is growing or when it is experiencing financial crisis, it may pay more attention to the statement of cash flows than to the income statement.

You have completed Part 9 of this program. If you think you understand the material in this part, you should now take Post Test 9, which is in the separate booklet. If you are uncertain about your understanding, you should review Part 9.

The post test will serve both to test your comprehension and to review the highlights of Part 9. After taking the post test, you may find that you are unsure about certain points. You should review these points before going on to Part 10.

2-56. On January 9, Glendale Market purchased a one-year insurance policy for $200, paying cash. (Recall that the right to insurance protection is an asset. For this asset, use the term "Prepaid Insurance.")

Change the following January 8 balance sheet so that it reports the financial condition on January 9.

GLENDALE MARKET
Balance Sheet as of January 8

Assets		Liabilities & Equity	
Cash	$14,100	Accounts payable	$ 2,000
Accounts receivable	900	Note payable	5,000
Inventory	2,700	Paid-in capital	10,000
		Retained earnings	700
Total	$17,700	Total	$17,700

GLENDALE MARKET
Balance Sheet as of January 8̶ 9

Assets		Liabilities & Equity	
Cash	**13,900** $̶1̶4̶,̶1̶0̶0̶	Accounts payable	$ 2,000
Accounts receivable	900	Note payable	5,000
Inventory	2,700	Paid-in capital	10,000
Pre-paid insurance 200		Retained earnings	700
Total	$17,700	Total	$17,700

2-57. On January 10, Glendale Market purchased two lots of land of equal size for a total of $10,000. It thereby acquired an asset, Land. It paid $2,000 in cash and gave a ten-year mortgage for the balance of $8,000. (Use the term "Mortgage Payable" for the liability.)

Change the following January 9 balance sheet so that it reports the financial condition on January 10.

GLENDALE MARKET
Balance Sheet as of January 9

Assets		Liabilities & Equity	
Cash	$13,900	Accounts payable	$ 2,000
Accounts receivable	900	Note payable	5,000
Inventory	2,700		
Prepaid insurance	200	Paid-in capital	10,000
		Retained earnings	700
Total	$17,700	Total	$17,700

GLENDALE MARKET
Balance Sheet as of January 8̶10

Assets		Liabilities & Equity	
Cash	**11,900** $̶1̶3̶,̶9̶0̶0̶	Accounts payable	$ 2,000
Accounts receivable	900	Note payable	5,000
Inventory	2,700	**Mortgage payable 8,000**	
Prepaid insurance	200	Paid-in capital	10,000
Land 10,000		Retained earnings	700
Total	$̶1̶7̶,̶7̶0̶0̶ **25,700**	Total	$̶1̶7̶,̶7̶0̶0̶ **25,700**

9-61. When a company is in financial difficulty, it may pay . . . [more / less] attention to its cash flow statement than to its income statement. It pays bills with cash—not net income.

more

9-62. Lenders want to know if cash flows are adequate to pay i _____ t on debt and to repay the p _____ when it becomes due.

interest   principal

9-63. Similarly, shareholders want to know about the adequacy of cash flow to pay d __ __ __ __ __ __ __ s.

dividends

> **NOTE:** A number that is useful for these purposes is called **Free Cash Flow.** It is calculated by subtracting from the cash flow expected from operating activities: (1) the cash needed to purchase normal fixed asset replacements, (2) the cash required to pay long-term debt that is coming due, and (3) normal dividend payments. The difference indicates the amount, if any, that the company is likely to have available (1) to provide a cushion against unforeseen cash outflows and (2) to provide for other spending that it might like to undertake.

KEY POINTS TO REMEMBER

- A required financial statement, the Statement of Cash Flows, reports the changes in balance sheet accounts as positive or negative impacts on cash during the accounting period.

- The statement has three sections: cash flow from operating activities, cash flow from investing activities, and cash flow from financing activities.

- The cash flow from operating activities is found by adjusting net income for (1) depreciation expense and (2) changes in noncash current assets and current liabilities.

- Depreciation expense is not a cash flow. Because it decreases net income, it is added back to net income in order to arrive at the cash flow from operating activities.

- In general, investing activities include the acquisition of new fixed assets and the proceeds of selling fixed assets.

- In general, financing activities include obtaining funds from long-term borrowing, repayment of these borrowings, and obtaining funds from issuance of additional stock.

2-58. On January 11, Glendale Market sold one of the two lots of land for $5,000. The buyer paid $1,000 cash and assumed $4,000 of the mortgage; that is, Glendale Market was no longer responsible for this half of the mortgage payable.

Change the following January 10 balance sheet so that it reports the financial condition on January 11.

GLENDALE MARKET
Balance Sheet as of January 10

Assets		Liabilities & Equity	
Cash	$11,900	Accounts payable	$ 2,000
Accounts receivable	900	Note payable	5,000
Inventory	2,700	Mortgage payable	8,000
Prepaid insurance	200	Paid-in capital	10,000
Land	10,000	Retained earnings	700
Total	$25,700	Total	$25,700

GLENDALE MARKET
Balance Sheet as of January ~~10~~ 11

Assets		Liabilities & Equity	
Cash	**12,900** ~~$11,900~~	Accounts payable	$ 2,000
Accounts receivable	900	Note payable	5,000
Inventory	2,700	Mortgage payable	**4,000** ~~8,000~~
Prepaid insurance	200	Paid-in capital	10,000
Land	**5,000** ~~10,000~~	Retained earnings	700
Total	~~$25,700~~ **21,700**	Total	~~$25,700~~ **21,700**

2-59. On January 12, Smith received an offer of $15,000 for his equity in Glendale Market. Although his equity was then only $10,700, he rejected the offer. This means that the store had already acquired goodwill with a market value of $4,300.

What changes, if any, should be made in the January 11 balance sheet so that it reports the financial condition on January 12? _____

_____

The balance sheet is unchanged from that of January 11, except for the date. In accordance with the asset measurement concept, goodwill is an asset only when it has been paid for. The balance sheet does not usually show the *fair value* of the entity.

> **NOTE:** Generally Accepted Accounting Principles (GAAP) classify other types of cash flows as either investing or financing. The investing category includes both making investments and disposition of investments; for example, sale of an item of plant is classified as an investing activity, as is the acquisition of an item of plant. Similarly, the financing category includes the repayment of borrowings, as well as cash received from loans. Because the statement of cash flows shows how each item is classified, users do not need to memorize these GAAP rules.

9-57. An investing activity . . . [is / is not] always a cash outflow, and a financing activity . . . [is / is not] always a cash inflow.

is not
is not

COMPLETING THE STATEMENT OF CASH FLOWS

9-58. Calculate the increase in cash by summing the three categories in Exhibit 11, and enter this total. Note that the $_____,000 net increase in cash . . . [equals / does not equal] the change in the Cash balance as reported on the two balance sheets of Arlen Company.

13
equals

9-59. The cash flow statement shows that although net income was $_____,000 in 2002, Cash increased by only $_____,000. Operating activities generated $_____,000 in cash; $_____,000 of this cash was used to pay dividends. The remaining additional cash inflow was used to acquire new Plant. The cost of the new assets was $_____,000; $_____,000 of this cost was financed by additional borrowing, and cash was used for the remainder. From the cash inflows, $_____,000 remained in the Cash account.

24 13
29 10

12

6

13

USES OF THE STATEMENT OF CASH FLOWS

9-60. A forecast of cash flows helps management and other users of financial information to estimate future needs for cash. For example, when a company is growing, the increase in its accounts receivables, inventory, and fixed assets may require . . . [more / less] cash. Therefore, although growth may result in additional profits, it may . . . [generate the need for / provide] additional cash.

more
generate the need for

2-60. On January 13, Smith withdrew for his personal use $200 cash from the Glendale Market bank account, and he also withdrew merchandise costing $400.

Change the following January 12 balance sheet so that it shows the financial condition on January 13.

GLENDALE MARKET
Balance Sheet as of January 12

Assets		Liabilities & Equity	
Cash	$12,900	Accounts payable	$ 2,000
Accounts receivable	900	Note payable	5,000
Inventory	2,700	Mortgage payable	4,000
Prepaid insurance	200	Paid-in capital	10,000
Land	5,000	Retained earnings	700
Total	$21,700	Total	$21,700

GLENDALE MARKET
Balance Sheet as of January ~~12~~ 13

Assets		Liabilities & Equity	
Cash	**12,700** ~~$12,900~~	Accounts payable	$ 2,000
Accounts receivable	900	Note payable	5,000
Inventory	**2,300** ~~2,700~~	Mortgage payable	4,000
Prepaid insurance	200	Paid-in capital	10,000
Land	5,000	Retained earnings	**100** ~~700~~
Total	~~$21,700~~ **21,100**	Total	~~$21,700~~ **21,100**

2-61. On January 14, Smith learned that the person who purchased the land on January 11 for $5,000, sold it for $8,000. The lot still owned by Glendale Market was identical in value with this other plot.

What changes, if any, should be made in the January 13 balance sheet so that it reports the financial condition on January 14? _____

_____

None. The balance sheet is identical to that of January 13, except for the date. As required by the asset-measurement concept, the land continues to be shown at its historical cost because it is a nonmonetary asset.

9-53. As shown in Exhibit 10, Arlen Company had a liability, mortgage bonds. The amount was $_____,000 at the beginning of 2002 and $_____,000 at the end of 2002. The increase of $_____,000 showed that Arlen Company issued bonds of this amount. This was a(n) . . . [investing / financing] activity. It represented a(n) . . . [increase / decrease] in cash. Enter this amount in Exhibit 11.

34

40   6

financing

increase

> **NOTE:** Similar to the transaction in Frame 9-50, the amount of new bonds issued may have been more than $6,000. Part of the new issue may have been used to pay off existing bonds. The issuance and redemption of bonds are financing activities.

9-54. The borrowings reported in the financing section are both short-term and long-term borrowings. Whereas short-term borrowings often appear as current liabilities, changes in them are reported in the section on Cash Flow from F _____ A _____.

Financing Activities

> **NOTE:** For example, the current portion of long-term debt is a current liability. For the purpose of cash flow analysis, it is reported as a financing activity.

9-55. Issuance of additional shares of a company's stock is also a financing activity. Exhibit 10 shows that Arlen Company's Paid-in Capital was $_____ at the beginning of 2002 and $_____ at the end of 2002. Evidently, the company . . . [did / did not] issue additional stock in 2002.

$60,000 $60,000

did not

9-56. Dividends paid are classified as a financing activity. Exhibit 10 shows that Arlen Company paid $_____,000 of dividends in 2002. Enter this amount in Exhibit 11. Then enter the total of the financing activities in Exhibit 11.

10

2-62. On January 15, Glendale Market paid off $2,000 of its bank loan, giving cash (disregard interest).

Change the following January 14 balance sheet so that it reports the financial condition on January 15.

GLENDALE MARKET
Balance Sheet as of January 14

Assets		Liabilities & Equity	
Cash	$12,700	Accounts payable	$ 2,000
Accounts receivable	900	Note payable	5,000
Inventory	2,300	Mortgage payable	4,000
Prepaid insurance	200	Paid-in capital	10,000
Land	5,000	Retained earnings	100
Total	$21,100	Total	$21,100

GLENDALE MARKET
Balance Sheet as of January ~~14~~ 15

Assets		Liabilities & Equity	
Cash	**10,700** ~~$12,700~~	Accounts payable	$ 2,000
Accounts receivable	900	Note payable	**3,000** ~~5,000~~
Inventory	2,300	Mortgage payable	4,000
Prepaid insurance	200	Paid-in capital	10,000
Land	5,000	Retained earnings	100
Total	~~$21,100~~ **19,100**	Total	~~$21,100~~ **19,100**

2-63. On January 16, Glendale Market was changed to a corporation. John Smith received 100 shares of common stock in exchange for his $10,100 equity in the business. He immediately sold 25 of these shares for $4,000 cash.

What changes, if any, should be made in the January 15 balance sheet so that it reports the financial condition on January 16? _____

_____

> **NOTE:** Any conceivable transaction can be recorded in terms of its effect on the balance sheet, just as you have done in this section. Although we shall describe techniques, refinements, and shortcuts in later parts, none of them changes this basic fact.

None. There is no change, except for the date. Changing the organization to a corporation did not affect any amount on the balance sheet. (The name of the entity was changed to, say, Glendale Market Corporation, but this does not affect the numbers.) John Smith's sale of the stock did not affect the entity, Glendale Market.

CASH FLOW FROM INVESTING AND FINANCING ACTIVITIES

9-48. Exhibit 11 shows that in addition to cash flow from operating activities, there are two other categories on a statement of cash flows: cash flow from _____ activities and cash flow from _____ activities.

investing

financing

9-49. When a company invests in additional property or plant, the amount involved is a cash . . . [inflow to / outflow from] the company.

outflow from

> **NOTE:** The amount may not be an immediate decrease in cash because the payment of cash may have been offset by borrowing an equal amount. Nevertheless, it is recorded as a cash outflow, and the amount of the borrowing is recorded separately as a financing activity.

9-50. As shown in Exhibit 10, Arlen Company had Plant at the beginning of 2002 that had cost $_____,000. It had $_____,000 of Plant at the end of 2002. The increase of $_____,000 was a(n) . . . [investing / financing] activity in 2002. Enter this amount in Exhibit 11. (The parentheses indicate that this was a cash outflow.)

108   120

12   investing

> **NOTE:** The amount of new plant acquired may have been more than $12,000, say $15,000; the difference of $3,000 would represent cash obtained from the sale of existing plant. Both transactions are investing activities. However, we cannot obtain a breakdown of the amount from the available information. Organizations often provide this breakdown for us on the statement of cash flows or elsewhere in the notes to their financial statements.

9-51. Similarly, if the Plant account decreased, representing the sale of plant assets, there would have been an . . . [inflow / outflow] of cash.

inflow

9-52. Companies may obtain cash by issuing debt securities, such as bonds. Issuing debt securities is a(n) . . . [investing / financing] activity.

financing

INCOME MEASUREMENT

Please turn to Exhibit 2 in your booklet. It is a summary of the transactions for Glendale Market that you analyzed in Frames 2-33 through 2-55. We shall focus on the transactions that affected Equity.

2-64. As explained in Part 1, an entity's equity increases for either of two reasons. One is the receipt of capital from owners. On January 2, Glendale Market received $10,000 from John Smith, its owner. You recorded this as an increase in _____ and an increase in the equity item, P _____ - _____ C _____.

Cash

Paid-in Capital

2-65. The other source of an increase in equity is the profitable operation of the entity. Transactions that increase profit also increase the equity item, R _____ E _____. Refer to the transactions for January 3 through 8. In the following table, show the dollar amount of the change in Retained Earnings, if any, that resulted from each transaction. If the transaction had no effect on Retained Earnings, put an X in the "No effect" column.

Retained Earnings

RETAINED EARNINGS

Date	Nature	Increased by	No effect
3	Borrowing	$	
4	Purchase		
5	Sale		
6	Purchase		
7	Sale		
8	Sale		
	Total	$	

RETAINED EARNINGS

Date	Nature	Increased by	No effect
3	Borrowing	$	X
4	Purchase		X
5	Sale	100	
6	Purchase		X
7	Sale	300	
8	Sale	300	
	Total	$ 700	

9-42. Note that the $_____$,000 adjustment for Depreciation Expense is . . . [larger than / smaller than / about the same as] the net amount of all the working capital account adjustments. This is the case in some companies, especially manufacturing companies, that have relatively large amounts of fixed assets.

6

larger than

9-43. As a shortcut, therefore, some analysts arrive at the operating cash flow simply by adding Depreciation Expense to Net Income. They disregard changes in the working capital accounts on the assumption that these changes net out to a minor amount. This shortcut may give the impression that depreciation is a cash flow. Such an impression is . . . [approximately correct / dead wrong]. Also, since the statement of cash flows is a required financial statement, it is a good idea to read it and obtain the operating cash flow information directly from it.

dead wrong

SUMMARY OF OPERATING ADJUSTMENTS

9-44. If the total amount of working capital (excluding cash) did not change, and if there are no noncash expenses, such as depreciation, cash flow from operations will be . . . [lower than / the same as / higher than] net income.

the same as

9-45. If the net amount of the working capital accounts (excluding cash) decreased, cash flow from operations will be . . . [lower than / higher than] net income.

higher than

9-46. If the net amount of the working capital accounts (excluding cash) increased, cash flow from operations will be . . . [lower than / higher than] net income.

lower than

9-47. If there was depreciation expense, cash flow from operations will be . . . [lower than / the same as / higher than] net income.

higher than

> **NOTE:** When analyzing the impact on cash from changes in working capital accounts, we must be careful to exclude the cash account from this calculation.

2-66. As can be seen from the table in Frame 2-65, three of these transactions did not affect Retained Earnings. Borrowing money . . . [does /
does not] affect Retained Earnings. The purchase of merchandise . . .
[does / does not] affect Retained Earnings. The sale of that merchandise,
however, . . . [does / does not] affect Retained Earnings.

does not

does not
does

2-67. The amount by which equity increased as a result of operations
during a period of time is called the **income** of that period. You have just
calculated that the total increase during the period January 2 through 8
was $_____, so Glendale Market's i _____ for that
period was $_____.

$700   income
$700

2-68. The amount of income and how it was earned is usually the most
important financial information about a business entity. An accounting
report called the **income statement** explains the income of a period.
Note that the income statement is for a . . . [period of time / point in
time], in contrast with the other statement, the b _____
s _____, which is for a . . . [period of time / point in time].

period of time

balance
sheet   point in time

2-69. The $700 increase in Retained Earnings during the period is re-
ported on the i _____ s _____. That state-
ment explains *why* this increase occurred.

income statement

2-70. To understand how the income statement does this, let's look at the
January 5 transaction for Glendale Market. On January 5, Glendale
Market sold for $300 cash some merchandise that had cost $200. This
caused equity (Retained Earnings) to . . . [increase / decrease] by
$_____.

increase
$100

2-71. On January 5, Glendale Market sold merchandise for $300 cash
that had cost $200. This transaction consists of two separate events:
(1) the sale, which, taken by itself, . . . [increased / decreased] Retained
Earnings by $300, and (2) the decrease in inventory, which, taken by it-
self, . . . [increased / decreased] Retained Earnings by $200.

increased

decreased

NET EFFECT OF WORKING CAPITAL CHANGES

9-38. In summary, an increase in current assets means that . . . [more /
less] of the cash inflow was tied up in accounts receivable, inventory,
and/or other current assets, with a corresponding . . . [increase / decrease]
in Cash. This is why, in times when cash is low, a business tries to keep
the other current assets as . . . [high / low] as feasible.

more

decrease

low

9-39. An increase in current liabilities means that . . . [more / less] cash
was freed up. The cash not paid to suppliers is still in the C _____ account. This is why, in times when cash is low, a business tries to keep
current liabilities as . . . [high / low] as feasible.

more

Cash

high

9-40. Users of financial statements need to understand these relationships, but there is no need to memorize them. The cash flow statement
gives the net effect of each of the four types of adjustments in working
capital items. Complete the following summary of them:

Change	Adjustment to Net Income	
Decrease in a current asset	add	
Increase in a current asset	[add / subtract]	subtract
Increase in a current liability	[add / subtract]	add
Decrease in a current liability	[add / subtract]	subtract

NOTE: Remember that these adjustments are made to convert the net income number to a cash basis. The net income number, as reported on the income statement, is *not changed.*

9-41. Complete the "Cash Flow from Operating Activities" section of
Exhibit 11. (Remember that numbers in parentheses are subtracted.) The
cash flow from operating activities was $_____,000.

29

2-72. Taken by itself, the increase in Retained Earnings resulting from operations is called a **revenue.** When Glendale Market sold merchandise for $300, the transaction resulted in $300 of _____.

revenue

2-73. And taken by itself, the associated decrease in Retained Earnings is called an **expense.** When Glendale Market transferred merchandise to the customer, the transaction reduced inventory and resulted in $200 of _____.

expense

2-74. Thus, when Glendale Market sold merchandise for $300 that cost $200, the effect of the transaction on Retained Earnings can be separated into two parts: a _____ of $_____ and an _____ of $_____.

revenue $300
expense $200

2-75. In accounting, revenues and expenses are recorded separately. From Exhibit 2, calculate the revenues and expenses for the period January 2 through 8 by completing the following table:

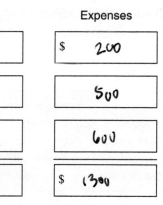

Date	Revenues	Expenses
5	$ 300	$ 200
7	800	500
8	900	600
Total	$ 2,000	$ 1,300

$ 300	$ 200
800	500
900	600
$2,000	$1,300

9-33. This follows from the fundamental accounting equation:

_____ = _____ + _____. To keep this equation in balance, a decrease in Accounts Receivable would necessarily mean an equal . . . [increase / decrease] in Cash, if these were the only two accounts involved.

Assets = Liabilities + Equity

increase

9-34. This makes sense because if everything else remains the same, a decrease in Accounts Receivable means more cash payments to the entity's C __ __ __ account.

Cash

> **NOTE:** A change in a current asset may not have an immediate effect on Cash. For example, an increase in Inventory may be accompanied by an increase in Accounts Payable. However, the ultimate effect on Cash for each separate transaction is as described, and the effect from the other accounts will be considered when we analyze those accounts.

ADJUSTMENTS FOR CHANGES IN CURRENT LIABILITIES

9-35. Changes in current liabilities have the opposite effect on Cash than changes in current assets. An increase in a current liability requires that the net income amount be adjusted to a cash basis by . . . [adding to it / subtracting from it]. A decrease in a current liability requires that the adjustment be a(n) . . . [addition / subtraction].

adding to it

subtraction

9-36. Exhibit 10 shows that Accounts Payable . . . [increased / decreased] by $_____,000. Therefore, net income is adjusted to a cash basis by . . . [adding / subtracting] this amount. Enter this change in Exhibit 11.

decreased

3

subtracting

9-37. Exhibit 10 shows that Accrued Wages . . . [increased / decreased] by $_____,000. Therefore, net income is adjusted to a cash basis by . . . [adding / subtracting] this amount. Enter this change in Exhibit 11.

increased

4

adding

2-76. You can now prepare an income statement. Its heading shows the name of the accounting entity, the title of the statement, and the period covered. Complete the heading for Glendale Market's income statement for January 2–8:

GLENDALE MARKET

INC   Statement

for the period   ｲ２ – １/８

Income

January 2–8

2-77. The income statement reports revenues and expenses for the period and the difference between them, which is income. Label the amounts in the following income statement for Glendale Market.

GLENDALE MARKET

Income Statement
for the period January 2–8

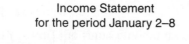

REV $2,000

EXP 1,300

INC .... $ 700

Revenues

Expenses

Income

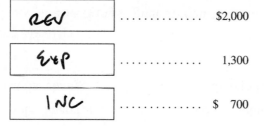

Revenues	$2,000

=

Expenses	$1,300	+	Income	$700

2-78. As the name suggests, Retained Earnings refers to the amount of income that has been r _____ in the entity. On January 13, Smith withdrew $600 of assets for his personal use. This reduced R _____ E _____ by $_____.

retained

Retained Earnings $600

9-27. Because the increase in Cash was . . . [more than / less than] the amount of Revenues, we must . . . [add to / subtract from] net income the amount that Cash was greater than Revenues. As shown above, this was $_____,000. Enter this amount in Exhibit 11.

more than
add to

2

9-28. If Accounts Receivable had increased during the period, the adjustment of net income would be the opposite; that is, an increase in a noncash current asset leads to an adjustment that . . . [adds to / subtracts from] net income in order to find the cash flow from operations.

subtracts from

9-29. As shown in Exhibit 10, the beginning balance in Inventory was $_____,000, and the ending balance was $_____,000, which shows that this asset . . . [increased / decreased] by $_____,000 during the year. This change had the opposite effect on Cash than the change in Accounts Receivable. Therefore, we must . . . [add to / subtract from] net income to arrive at the change in cash. Enter the $4,000 in Exhibit 11.

56   60
increased   4

subtract from

9-30. If the balance in a working capital account is unchanged, the inflow to Cash . . . [is / is not] the same amount as revenue, and an adjustment . . . [is / is not] necessary.

is
is not

9-31. To summarize, we must analyze changes in the balance sheet accounts to determine their impact on Cash. We are interested in the w _____ c _____ accounts to prepare the "cash flows from o _ _ _ _ _ _ _ _ activities" section of the statement of cash flows.

working capital
operating

9-32. An easy way to remember whether the impact on Cash (and hence the adjustment to net income) is an addition or a subtraction is to pretend that only that one account and Cash exist. For example, if Cash and Accounts Receivable were the only accounts, a decrease in Accounts Receivable would have to mean a(n) . . . [increase / decrease] in Cash.

increase

2-79. No other changes in Retained Earnings occurred. Complete the following table:

Retained Earnings, January 2	$ 0	
Income	+ _700_	700
Withdrawal	− _600_	600
Retained Earnings, January 13	$ _100_	100

The amount of Retained Earnings calculated . . . [does / does not] equal the amount shown on the balance sheet of January 13.

does

2-80. Assume that in the remainder of January, Glendale Market had additional income of $800 and there were no additional withdrawals. Since Retained Earnings was $100 as of January 13, it would be $_900_ on January 31. Thus, the amount of Retained Earnings on a balance sheet is:

$900

   A. the amount earned in the current period.

   B. the total amount retained since the entity began operations.

B

2-81. The terms **profit, earnings, surplus,** and **income** all have the same meaning. They are the differences between the r _evenues_ of an accounting period and the e _xpenses_ of that period.

revenues

expenses

> **NOTE:** Some people use the term **income** when they mean **revenue;** this can be confusing.

> **NOTE:** In later parts, we shall describe various revenue and expense items, such as sales revenue, interest revenue, salary expense, and rent expense. These explain in more detail the reasons for the change in Retained Earnings during a period.

2-82. Remember that the Equity section of the balance sheet reports the amount of capital that the entity has obtained from two different sources:

   1. The amount paid in by the owner(s), which is called P _aid_ - _in_ C _apital_ .

Paid-in Capital

   2. The amount of income that has been retained in the entity, which is called R _et_ E _arnings_ .

Retained Earnings

9-24. Consider what the account balances would have been if Arlen Company had revenue of $300,000 but had received $302,000 cash from customers. Enter the $302,000 in the T-accounts shown below and find the account balances.

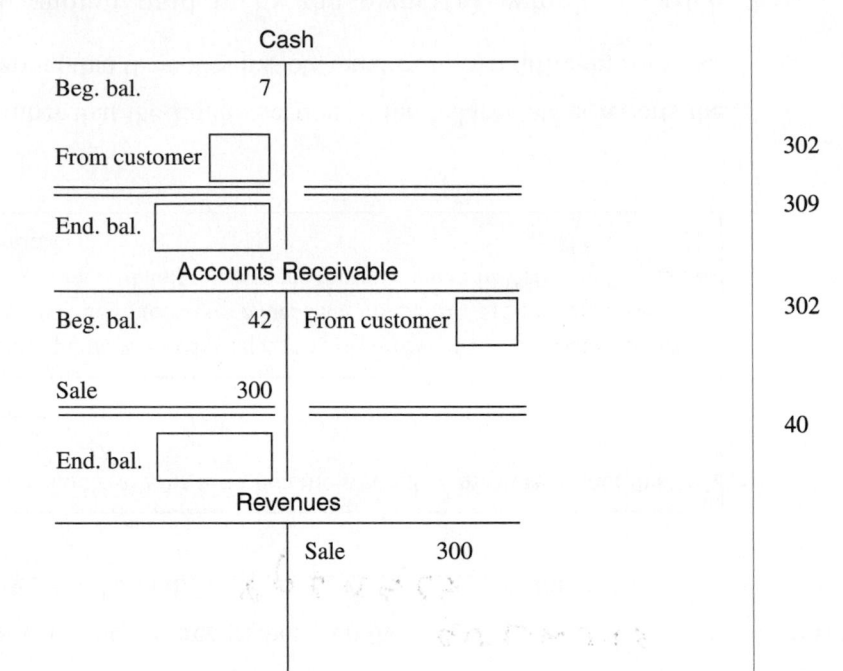

Cash

Beg. bal.	7	
From customer	☐	
End. bal.	☐	

Accounts Receivable

Beg. bal.	42	From customer	☐
Sale	300		
End. bal.	☐		

Revenues

| | | Sale | 300 |

302

309

302

40

9-25. The above accounts show that in this situation, the ending balance of Cash would have been . . . [$2,000 larger than / $2,000 smaller than / the same as] the Cash balance when cash receipts equaled sales revenues, as shown in Frame 9-22. The Accounts Receivable balance would have been . . . [$2,000 larger than / $2,000 smaller than / the same as] the balance when cash receipts equaled sales revenues. Revenues in 2002 would still have been $300,000.

$2,000 larger than

$2,000 smaller than

9-26. This example shows that if the ending balance in Accounts Receivable was *less* than its beginning balance, the increase in Cash would be . . . [more than / less than / the same as] the amount of Revenues. Part of the increase in Cash would be the result of decreasing Accounts Receivable. Put another way, Cash increased partly because more old customers paid their bills and partly because of sales to new customers. This is what happened in Arlen Company.

more than

2-83. The two financial statements may be compared to two reports on a reservoir. One report may show how much water *flowed through* the reservoir during the period, and the other report may show how much water *was in* the reservoir as of the end of the period. Similarly, the . . . [balance sheet / income statement] reports flows during a period of time, whereas the . . . [balance sheet / income statement] reports status as of a point of time.

income statement

balance sheet

Thus, the income statement may be called a . . . [flow / status] report, and the balance sheet may be called a . . . [flow / status] report.

flow

status

2-84. Note also that withdrawals by owners (which are called dividends in a corporation) . . . [are / are not] expenses. They . . . [do / do not] appear on the income statement. They . . . [do / do not] reduce income. They . . . [do / do not] decrease retained earnings.

are not   do not

do not

do

KEY POINTS TO REMEMBER

The following diagram summarizes how assets are reported.

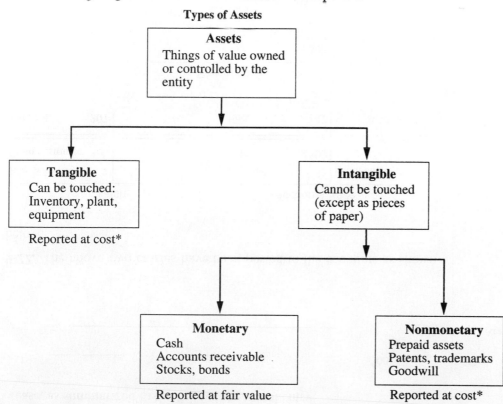

Types of Assets

Assets
Things of value owned or controlled by the entity

Tangible
Can be touched: Inventory, plant, equipment

Reported at cost*

Intangible
Cannot be touched (except as pieces of paper)

Monetary
Cash
Accounts receivable
Stocks, bonds

Reported at fair value

Nonmonetary
Prepaid assets
Patents, trademarks
Goodwill

Reported at cost*

---

*Historical cost less depreciation or amortization

9-21. If, in 2002, Arlen Company received $300,000 cash from credit customers, Cash would increase and Accounts Receivable would decrease, as summarized in the following journal entry:

Dr. _____ 300   Cash

Cr. _____ _____ 300   Accounts Receivable

9-22. The above two entries have been posted to the accounts as shown below:

Cash		Accounts Receivable		
Beg. bal.	7	Beg. bal.	42	From customer 300
From customer 300		Sale	300	
End. bal.	307	End. bal.	42	

Revenues	
	Sale 300

As these accounts show, when the balance in Accounts Receivable does not change, the increase in cash is . . . [more than / less than / the same as] the sales revenue.

the same as

9-23. This is the case with all working capital accounts. If the beginning balance is the same as the ending balance, an adjustment from the accrual basis to the cash basis . . . [is / is not] necessary when preparing the statement of cash flows.

is not

- Current assets are cash and assets that are expected to be converted into cash or used up in the near future, usually within one year.

- Current liabilities are obligations due in the near future, usually within one year.

- Marketable securities are current assets; investments are noncurrent assets.

- A single liability may have both a current portion and a noncurrent portion.

- Equity consists of paid-in capital (which in a corporation is represented by shares of stock) plus earnings retained since the entity began. It does not report the market value of the stock. Retained earnings is not cash; it is part of the owners' claim on the assets.

- Every accounting transaction affects at least two items and preserves the basic equation: Assets = Liabilities + Equity. Accounting is a double-entry system.

- Some events are not transactions; they do not affect the accounting amounts. Examples in this part were: a change in the value of land, "goodwill" that was not purchased, and changing the entity from a proprietorship to a corporation.

- Other events affect assets and/or liabilities but have no effect on equity. Examples in this part were borrowing money, purchasing inventory, purchasing insurance protection, acquiring an asset, giving a mortgage, buying land, selling land at its cost, and repaying a bank loan.

- Still other events affect equity as well as assets and/or liabilities. Revenues are increases in equity resulting from operations during a period. Expenses are decreases. Their net effect is shown in the equity item called Retained Earnings. Equity also increases when owners pay in capital, and equity decreases when owners withdraw capital, but these transactions do not affect income.

- A sale has two aspects: a revenue aspect and an expense aspect. Revenue results when the sale is made, whether or not cash is received at that time. The related expense is the cost of the merchandise that was sold. The income of a period is the difference between the revenues and expenses of that period.

You have completed Part 2 of this program. If you think you understand the material in this part, you should now take Post Test 2, which is in the separate booklet. If you are uncertain about your understanding, you should review Part 2.

The post test will serve both to test your comprehension and to review the highlights of Part 2. After taking the post test, you may find that you are unsure about certain points. You should review these points before going on to Part 3.

ADJUSTMENTS FOR CHANGES IN WORKING CAPITAL ACCOUNTS

9-17. Cash, accounts receivable, inventory, and similar items that will be converted into cash in the near future are c _____ assets. Accounts payable, wages payable, and similar obligations that are due in the near future are c _____ liabilities. The difference between current assets and current liabilities is called **working capital.** Operating activities—such as making sales; purchasing materials for inventory; and incurring production, selling, and administrative expenses—are the principal causes of changes in working capital items. We shall analyze the asset and liability categories separately.

current

current

> **NOTE:** Although cash is, of course, an item of working capital, we exclude it here when we adjust for changes in working capital accounts because we want to analyze the impact of such changes on cash.

ADJUSTMENTS FOR CHANGES IN CURRENT ASSETS

9-18. If all revenues in 2002 were from cash sales, cash inflows . . . [would / would not] be the same amount as revenues; that is, if sales revenues were $300,000, cash inflows would be $_____,000. However, in most companies, some sales are made to credit customers. These sales are first reported as the current asset, A __ __ __ __ __ __ __ R __ __ __ __ __ __ __ __ __ __ . The company will receive cash later on, when customers pay their bills.

would

300

Accounts
Receivable

9-19. In Arlen Company, all sales were credit sales. If sales in 2002 were $300,000, Revenues would be $_____,000, and Accounts Receivable would increase by $_____,000 when these sales were made.

300

300

9-20. The journal entry summarizing the above transaction would be (omitting 000):

Dr. A _____ R _____   300

Cr. R _____   300

Accounts Receivable

Revenues

Part 3

Accounting Records and Systems

Learning Objectives

In this part you will learn:

- The nature of the account and how entries are made to accounts.
- The meaning of debit and credit.
- Use of the ledger and the journal.
- The closing process.
- Items reported on the income statement.
- Accounting with the computer.

THE ACCOUNT

3-1. In Part 2 you recorded the effect of each transaction by changing the appropriate items on a balance sheet. Erasing the old amounts and writing in the new amounts . . . [would / would not] be a practical method for handling the large number of transactions that occur in most entities.

would not

3-2. Instead of changing balance sheet amounts directly, accountants use a device called an **account** to record each change. In its simplest form, an account looks like a large letter T, and it is therefore called a _____ -account.

T

> **NOTE:** As a matter of accounting custom, the name of an account is treated as a proper noun; that is, the first letter is capitalized.

9-13. If Depreciation expense was $4,000 higher than the amount reported in Exhibit 10, Net income would be $4,000 . . . [higher than / lower than / the same as] the amount reported. The $4,000 increase in Depreciation expense would offset exactly the $4,000 decrease in Net income. Cash flow would be . . . [higher than / lower than / the same as] the amount reported in Exhibit 11.

lower than

the same as

9-14. To reinforce this point, recall the journal entry that records Depreciation Expense:

Dr. D _____ E _____

Depreciation Expense

Cr. A _____ D _____

Accumulated Depreciation

The Cash account . . . [was / was not] changed by this entry.

was not

9-15. To repeat, the cash for fixed assets was paid out when the fixed assets were purchased (or when borrowings made in connection with such a purchase were paid back). Cash . . . [is / is not] affected by the depreciation charge; to do so would be double counting.

is not

> **NOTE:** Amortization of intangible assets, write-off of losses, and other non-cash expenses also are added to net income to convert net income to cash flow from operating activities.

9-16. Thus, depreciation . . . [is / is not] a source of cash. (This is a common misconception because of the role it plays on the statement of cash flows to adjust net income to a cash basis.)

is not

3-3. The title of the account is written on top of the T. Draw a T-account and title it "Cash."

```
                Cash
_____
              |
              |
              |
              |
```

3-4. Following is how a T-account looks at the beginning of an accounting period.

```
                Cash
_____
  Beg. bal. 10,000  |
                    |
                    |
                    |
```

Evidently the amount of cash at the beginning of the accounting period was $_____.

$10,000

(Note that although the amounts are in dollars, the dollar sign is not used.)

3-5. Transactions that affect the Cash account during the accounting period can either **increase** cash or **decrease** cash. Thus, one side of the T-account is for __ __ __ __ __ __ __ __ __ s, and the other side is for __ __ __ __ __ __ __ __ __ s.

increases

decreases (either order)

3-6. Increases in cash add to the beginning balance. Because the beginning balance is recorded on the left side of the T-account, increases in cash are recorded on the . . . [left / right] side of the T-account. Decreases are recorded on the . . . [left / right] side.

left

right

9-8. Net income is the difference between r __ __ __ __ __ es and | revenues
e __ __ __ __ __ es. "Cash flow from operating activities" is the differ- | expenses
ence between **operating** cash inflows and **operating** cash outflows. To
find the amount of cash flow from operating activities, we must make
two types of adjustments to net income: (1) for depreciation and other
expenses that will not *ever* require an outflow of c __ __ __ and (2) for | cash
changes in working capital accounts (accounts that are an integral part of
daily operating activities).

ADJUSTMENT FOR DEPRECIATION EXPENSE

9-9. According to its balance sheet (Exhibit 10), Arlen Company owned
Plant, most of which it had acquired . . . [prior to / in] the year 2002 at a | prior to
cost of $_____,000. The cash outflow for these assets occurred . . . | 108
[prior to 2002 / in 2002]. | prior to 2002

9-10. According to its income statement, Arlen Company had a
Depreciation expense of $_____,000 in 2002. Depreciation recognizes a | 6
portion of the cost of fixed assets. The cash outflow for the assets on hand
at the beginning of 2002 occurred in earlier years; this Depreciation ex-
pense therefore . . . [was / was not] a cash outflow in 2002. | was not

9-11. Although Depreciation expense is subtracted from Revenue in arriving at Net income, it is not a cash outflow. Net income is $6,000 less
than it would have been with no Depreciation expense. Therefore, Net in-
come is adjusted to a cash basis by . . . [adding $6,000 to / subtracting | adding $6,000 to
$6,000 from] Net income. Enter this adjustment in Exhibit 11.

9-12. Suppose that Arlen Company had decided to recognize
Depreciation expense of $10,000, rather than $6,000, in 2002 but made
no other changes in the accounts. The cash flow from operating activities
would then be . . . [higher than / lower than / the same as] the amount re- | the same as
ported in Exhibit 11.

NOTE: If you answered Frame 9-12 correctly, go to Frame 9-14.

3-7. Here is the T-account for Cash.

	Cash	
	(Increases)	(Decreases)
	Beg. bal. 10,000	

Record in the above T-account the effect of the following transactions on Cash:

A. The entity received $300 cash from a customer.

B. The entity borrowed $5,000 from a bank.

C. The entity paid $2,000 cash to a supplier.

D. The entity sold merchandise for $800 cash.

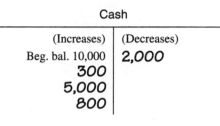

	Cash	
	(Increases)	(Decreases)
	Beg. bal. 10,000	**2,000**
	300	
	5,000	
	800	

3-8. At the end of an accounting period, the increases are added to the beginning balance, and the total of the decreases is subtracted from it. The result is the **new balance.** Calculate the new balance for the Cash account shown below.

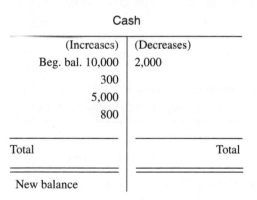

	Cash		
	(Increases)	(Decreases)	
	Beg. bal. 10,000	2,000	
	300		
	5,000		
	800		
Total		Total	
New balance			

	Cash		
	(Increases)	(Decreases)	
	Beg. bal. 10,000	2,000	
	300		
	5,000		
	800		
Total	**16,100**	**2,000**	Total
New balance			
	14,100		

3-9. The amount of the above Cash shown on the balance sheet at the end of the accounting period was $_____. The beginning balance of Cash in the next accounting period will be $_____.

$14,100

$14,100

9-6. The indirect method analyzes the income statement and balance sheet account *changes* to determine whether such changes had a positive or negative impact on c __ __ __ f __ __ __ . Since the balance sheet must always stay in balance, it is easy to determine the impact on c _____ by analyzing changes in each of the other accounts.

cash flow

cash

9-7. In preparing the statement of cash flows, we are interested in **changes** in the balance sheet accounts from one accounting period to another. The purpose of the statement of cash flows is to provide information about items that caused the c __ __ __ __ __ in cash from one balance sheet to another. This will help us to understand the **sources** and **uses** of cash during the accounting period.

change

> **NOTE:** We next develop a statement of cash flows for Arlen Company, using the indirect method and the balance sheet and income statement information in Exhibit 10.
>
> We will work with the statement of cash flows in Exhibit 11. It consists of three sections. We will describe the first section, called "cash flow from operating activities," in some detail. We will describe the other two sections, called "cash flow from investing activities" and "cash flow from financing activities," together because the same principles apply to both. The principal purpose of this part is to show the relationship between the accrual accounting numbers and cash.

CASH FLOW FROM OPERATING ACTIVITIES

> **NOTE:** The first section of the statement of cash flows reports how much cash was generated by the operating activities of the period—the day-to-day activities that bring cash in from customers and pay cash out to employees and suppliers. To do this, we must first analyze the balance sheet accounts that contain information about the day-to-day operating activities. We need to focus first on the balance sheet accounts that are concerned with operating activities. We will then convert this information from an accrual basis to a cash basis.

RULES FOR INCREASES AND DECREASES

3-10. In the T-account for Cash, increases are recorded on the . . . [left / right] side. This is the rule for all asset accounts; that is, increases in _____ accounts are recorded on the _____ side.

left

asset   left

3-11. Suppose Brown Company received $300 cash from Ellen Jones to settle her account receivable. In the T-account below, the increase in Brown Company's cash that results is recorded on the . . . [left / right] side. Enter the amount.

left

Cash	
(Increases)	(Decreases)
Beg. bal. 10,000	
300	

Cash	
(Increases)	(Decreases)
Beg. bal. 10,000	
300	

3-12. Ellen Jones, a customer of Brown Company, paid $300 cash to settle the amount she owed. The Cash account increased by $300. Jones no longer owed $300, so the A 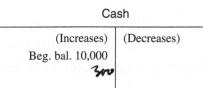 _ _ _ _ _ account decreased by $300. In the T-account below, enter the name of this second account that must be changed to complete the record of the transaction.

Accounts

Receivable

Cash			Accts Rec	
(Increases)	(Decreases)		(Increases)	(Decreases)
Beg. bal. 10,000			Beg. bal. 2,000	300
300				

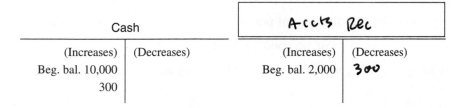

Accounts Receivable

3-13. Accounts Receivable is an asset account. The dual-aspect concept requires that if the asset account, Cash, increases by $300, the change in the other asset account, Accounts Receivable, must be a(n) . . . [increase / decrease] of $300.

decrease

9-3. Both the income statement and the cash flow statement report flows during the period. The difference is that the income statement reports flows on the **accrual** basis; that is, inflows are measured as r _____ s and outflows are measured as e _____ s. By contrast, the statement of cash flows reports inflows and outflows of c _____ .

revenues   expenses

cash

> **NOTE:** The income statement focuses on *profitability*. The statement of cash flows focuses on *liquidity* and *solvency*.

9-4. For example, assume that an entity sold goods for $1,000 on May 1, and the customer paid $1,000 for these goods on June 1. Its cash inflow on May 1 would be . . . [$0 / $1,000], and its revenue in May would be . . . [$0 / $1,000]. Its cash inflow on June 1 would be . . . [$0 / $1,000], and its revenue in June would be . . . [$0 / $1,000]. Its balance sheet at the end of May would include this $1,000 as an asset, called A _____ R _____ .

$0

$1,000 $1,000

$0

Accounts Receivable

> **NOTE:** Therefore, an entity's revenues and expenses in a period do not necessarily match its cash receipts and disbursements in that period. This is one of the most important concepts to understand in learning financial accounting.

9-5. There are two acceptable methods of preparing the statement of cash flows. One is to summarize the inflows and outflows to the Cash account **directly;** it is therefore called the d _ _ _ _ _ method. Most companies, however, use the other method, which is called the ind _ _ _ _ _ _ method.

direct

indirect

> **NOTE:** Companies that use the indirect method report their cash flows *indirectly* by adjusting net income to remove the effects of accrual accounting. The indirect method is much more widely used because it shows the relationship between the income statement and the balance sheet and therefore aids in the analysis of these statements.

3-14. Record the change in Accounts Receivable resulting from the $300 payment in the account below.

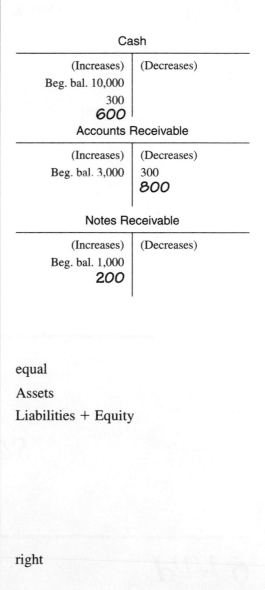

Accounts Receivable

(Increases)	(Decreases)
Beg. bal. 2,000	300

3-15. The decrease in accounts receivable was recorded on the . . . [left / right] side of the Accounts Receivable account. This balanced the . . . [left / right] -side amount for the increase in Cash.

right

left

3-16. Another customer of Brown Company settled an $800 Account Receivable by paying $600 Cash and giving a note for $200. Record this transaction in the Brown Company's accounts, given below.

Cash

(Increases)	(Decreases)
Beg. bal. 10,000	
300	
600	

Accounts Receivable

(Increases)	(Decreases)
Beg. bal. 3,000	300
	800

Notes Receivable

(Increases)	(Decreases)
Beg. bal. 1,000	
200	

3-17. As you can see, accounting requires that each transaction give rise to . . . [equal / unequal] totals of left-side and right-side amounts. This is consistent with the fundamental equation: A _ _ _ _ _ = L _ _ _ _ _ _ _ _ _ _ _ _ + E _ _ _ _ _ _ .

equal

Assets

Liabilities + Equity

3-18. An **increase** in any asset account is always recorded on the left side. Therefore, since the totals of left-side and right-side amounts must equal each other, a **decrease** in any asset must always be recorded on the . . . [left / right] side.

right

Part 9

Statement of Cash Flows

Learning Objectives

In this part you will learn:

- What a statement of cash flows is.
- How it differs from an income statement.
- The meaning of the term "cash flow from operations."
- The content of the other two sections.
- The relationship of depreciation to cash flow.
- Uses of the statement of cash flows.

9-1. A company must prepare three financial statements. We described two of them in earlier parts. The . . . [balance sheet / income statement] reports the financial status of the company as of the end of each accounting period. The . . . [balance sheet / income statement] reports financial performance during the period.

balance sheet

income statement

9-2. In this part, we describe the third required statement. It reports the **flow of cash** during the accounting period, and it is therefore called the statement of c _ _ _ f _ _ _ s.

cash flows

3-19. Black Company borrowed $700 from Federal Bank, signing a note.

Black Company's Cash account . . . [increased / decreased] by $700, and its Notes Payable account, which is a liability account, . . . [increased / decreased] by the same amount.

increased
increased

3-20. Black Company borrowed $700 from Federal Bank, signing a note.

The $700 increase in Black Company's cash is recorded on the . . . [left / right] side of its Cash account. In order to show equal totals of right-side and left-side amounts, the corresponding change in the Notes Payable account is recorded on the . . . [left / right] side. Record the two amounts of this transaction in the accounts below.

left

right

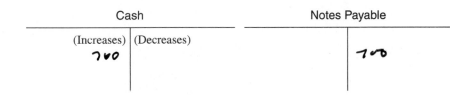

Cash		Notes Payable
(Increases)	(Decreases)	
700		700

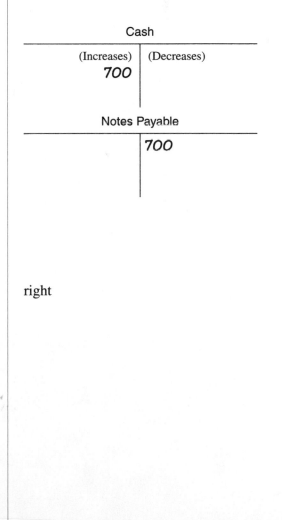

Cash	
(Increases)	(Decreases)
700	

Notes Payable
700

3-21. Because left-side and right-side amounts must have equal totals, and because increases in assets are always recorded on the left side, increases in liability accounts, such as Notes Payable, are always recorded on the . . . [left / right] side.

right

You have completed Part 8 of this program. If you think you understand the material in this part, you should now take Post Test 8, which is in the separate booklet. If you are uncertain about your understanding, you should review Part 8.

The post test will serve both to test your comprehension and to review the highlights of Part 8. After taking the post test, you may find that you are unsure about certain points. You should review these points before going on to Part 9.

3-22. Similarly, because **decreases** in assets are always recorded on the *right* side, **decreases** in liabilities are always recorded on the . . . [left side / right side].

left side

Show which side of the Notes Payable account is used to record increases and which side is used to record decreases by filling in the boxes below.

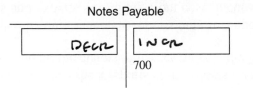

Notes Payable

DECR | INCR

700

Notes Payable

(Decreases)	(Increases)
	700

3-23. As the equation Assets = Liabilities + Equity indicates, the rules for equity accounts are the same as those for liability accounts, that is:

Equity accounts increase on the . . . [left / right] side.

right

Equity accounts decrease on the . . . [left / right] side.

left

3-24. One way to remember the above rules is to visualize the two sides of the balance sheet.

Asset accounts are on the *left* side of the balance sheet, and they increase on the . . . [left / right] side.

left

Liability and equity accounts are on the *right* side of the balance sheet, and they increase on the . . . [left / right] side.

right

3-25. The reasoning used in the preceding frames follows from the basic equation: _____ = _____ + _____ .

Assets = Liabilities + Equity

> **NOTE:** Sometimes you will see a balance sheet where liabilities and equity appear below the assets section. This is a matter of preference on the part of the reporting entity.

KEY POINTS TO REMEMBER

- A company obtains its permanent capital from two sources: (1) debt (i.e., noncurrent liabilities) and (2) equity. It uses this capital to finance (1) working capital (i.e., current assets – current liabilities) and (2) noncurrent assets.

- Most debt capital is obtained by issuing bonds. Bonds obligate the company to pay interest and to repay the principal when it is due.

- Equity capital is obtained by (1) issuing shares of stock and (2) retaining earnings.

- The amount of capital obtained from preferred and common shareholders is the amount they paid in. The par, or stated, value of common stock is not an important number today, but it is still reported on the balance sheet.

- Cash dividends decrease the amount of equity capital. Stock dividends or stock splits do not affect the total equity.

- Retained earnings are total earnings (i.e., net income) since the entity began operations, less total dividends. (A net loss, of course, results in a decrease in retained earnings.)

- Although sometimes called "net worth," the amount of owners' equity does *not* show what the owners' interest is worth.

- In deciding on its permanent capital structure, a company attempts to strike the right balance between (1) risky but low-cost debt capital and (2) less risky but high-cost equity capital. For a given company this balance is indicated by its debt ratio.

- Many companies have subsidiaries. The economic entity is a family consisting of the parent and the subsidiaries (in which, by definition, it owns more than 50% of the stock). Consolidated financial statements are prepared for such an economic entity by combining their separate financial statements and eliminating transactions among members of the family.

- The consolidated balance sheet reports all the assets owned by the consolidated entity and all the claims of parties outside the family.

- The consolidated income statement reports only revenues from sales to outside parties and expenses resulting from costs incurred with outside parties. Intrafamily revenues and expenses are eliminated.

DEBIT AND CREDIT

3-26. In the language of accounting, the left side of an account is called the **debit** side, and the right side is called the **credit** side. Thus, instead of saying that increases in cash are recorded on the left side of the Cash account and decreases are recorded on the right side, accountants say that increases are recorded on the _____debit_____ side and decreases are recorded on the _____credit_____ side.

debit

credit

3-27. Debit and **Credit** are also verbs. To record an increase in cash, you _____Debit_____ the Cash account. To record a decrease in cash, you _____Credit_____ the Cash account. Instead of saying, "Record an amount on the left side of the Cash account," the accountant simply says, "_____Debit_____ Cash."

debit

credit

Debit

3-28. Increases in all asset accounts, such as Cash, are recorded on the . . . [debit / credit] side. To increase an asset account, you . . . [debit / credit] the account.

debit   debit

3-29. The rules we just developed in terms of "left side" and "right side" can now be stated in terms of debit and credit.

Increases in assets are [debits / credits].

debits

Decreases in assets are [debits / credits].

credits

Increases in liabilities are [debits / credits].

credits

Decreases in liabilities are [debits / credits].

debits

Increases in equity are [debits / credits].

credits

Decreases in equity are [debits / credits].

debits

3-30. In everyday language the word **credit** sometimes means "good" and **debit** sometimes means "bad." In the language of accounting, debit means only . . . [left / right], and credit means only . . . [left / right].

left   right

> **NOTE:** As you can see from Frame 3-29, debits are sometimes increases (when asset accounts are involved) and sometimes decreases (when liability or equity accounts are involved).

8-74. Palm Company owns 60% of the stock of Sand Company. This stock was reported on the balance sheet of Palm Company as an asset, Investment in Subsidiaries, at $60,000. The total equity of Sand Corporation is $100,000. On the consolidated balance sheet, the $60,000 asset would be eliminated, and because debits must equal credits, . . . [$60,000 / $100,000] of Sand Company's consolidated equity also would be eliminated.

$60,000

8-75. Palm Company owns 60% of Sand Company's stock, which is a . . . [majority / minority] of the stock. Other shareholders own the other 40% of Sand Company stock; they are . . . [majority / minority] shareholders. They have an interest in the consolidated entity, and this interest is reported in the . . . [assets / liabilities and equity] side of the consolidated balance sheet. It is labeled **minority interest.**

majority
minority

liabilities and equity

8-76. The consolidated income statement reports revenues from . . . [all sales / sales to outside parties only] and expenses resulting from . . . [all costs incurred / costs incurred with outside parties]. Intrafamily revenues and expenses are e __ __ __ __ __ __ __ __ __ d.

sales to outside parties only
costs incurred with outside parties

eliminated

8-77. The consolidated financial statements report on the entity called "Palm Company and Subsidiaries." This family of corporations . . . [is / is not] an economic entity, but it . . . [is / is not] a legal entity.

is
is not

8-78. Many corporations have subsidiaries. Since the consolidated financial statements give the best information about the economic entity, many published financial statements are c __ __ __ __ __ __ __ __ __ __ __ d financial statements.

consolidated

> **NOTE:** In an entity with dozens of subsidiaries, some of which have their own subsidiaries, eliminating the intrafamily transactions is a complicated task. Only the general principles have been described here.

3-31. The word **debit** is abbreviated as "Dr.," and the word **credit** is abbreviated as "Cr." Label the two sides of the Cash account below with these abbreviations.

	Cash	
	DR	CR
Beg. bal. 1,000		

	Cash	
	(Dr.)	(Cr.)
Beg. bal. 1,000		

Debits   Credits

> **NOTE:** In practice, these labels are not shown in the accounts, but we shall use them in the next frames, to help you fix them in your mind.

3-32. Exhibit 3 (in your booklet) shows the accounts for Green Company, arranged as they would appear on a balance sheet. The sum of the debit balances is $_____18K_____, and the sum of the credit balances is $_____18K_____.

$18,000

$18,000

3-33. These totals are equal in accordance with the d _u a l_ - a _s p e c t_ concept.

dual-
aspect

8-70. In 2001, Palm Company had sales revenue of $1,000,000, Sea Company had sales revenue of $200,000, and Sand Company had sales revenue of $400,000. Palm Company sold $30,000 of products to Sea Company. All other sales were to outside customers. On the consolidated income statement, the amount of sales reported would be $_____.

$1,570,000
(Total sales = $1,000,000 + $200,000 + $400,000 = $1,600,000.
Intrafamily sales = $30,000.
Consolidated sales = $1,600,000 – $30,000 = $1,570,000.)

8-71. Intrafamily transactions are also eliminated from the consolidated balance sheet. For example, if Sand Company owed Palm Company $10,000, this amount would appear as Accounts . . . [Receivable / Payable] on the balance sheet of Palm Company and as Accounts . . . [Receivable / Payable] on the balance sheet of Sand Company. On the consolidated balance sheet, the Accounts Receivable and Accounts Payable would each be $10,000 . . . [more / less] than the sum of these amounts on the balance sheets of each of the family members.

Receivable

Payable

less

8-72. The balance sheet of Palm Company reports as an asset the Sand Company and Sea Company stock that it owns. This asset . . . [remains unchanged / must be eliminated] from the consolidated balance sheet. On the balance sheets of the subsidiaries, the corresponding amounts are reported as . . . [noncurrent liabilities / equity], and these amounts are also eliminated on the consolidated balance sheet.

must be eliminated

equity

8-73. Palm Company owns 40% of Gray Company stock. This asset is listed on Palm Company's balance sheet at $100,000. This asset would *not* be eliminated from the consolidated balance sheet. Why not?

Because only companies in which the parent owns more than 50% are consolidated.

3-34. Record the following transactions in the accounts of Exhibit 3. Record increases in assets on the debit side and make sure that in each transaction the debit and credit amounts are equal.

    A. Inventory costing $600 was purchased for cash.

    B. Inventory costing $400 was purchased on credit.

    C. Green Company paid $300 to a creditor.

    D. Green Company received $500 in cash from a credit customer.

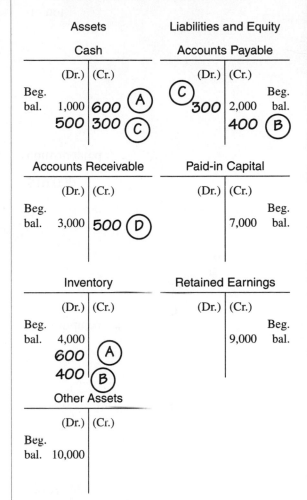

ACCOUNTS FOR GREEN COMPANY

3-35. Now calculate the new balances for each account and enter them in the accounts of Exhibit 3.

The new balances are:

Cash . . . . 600 Dr.
Accounts Receivable . . . . . 2,500 Dr.
Inventory . . . . 5,000 Dr.
Other Assets . . . . 10,000 Dr.
Accounts Payable . . . . 2,100 Cr.
Paid-in Capital . . . . 7,000 Cr.
Retained Earnings . . . . 9,000 Cr.

3-36. The total of the new balances of the asset accounts is $_____. The total of the new balances of the liability and equity accounts is $_____. Also, the total of the debit balances equals the total of the _____ balances.

$18,100

$18,100

credit

CONSOLIDATED FINANCIAL STATEMENTS

8-65. A corporation that controls one or more other corporations is called the **parent,** and the controlled corporations are called **subsidiaries.**

Palm Company owns 100% of the stock of Sea Company, 60% of the stock of Sand Company, and 40% of the stock of Gray Company. The **parent** company is _____ _____. The subsidiaries are _____ _____ and _____ _____.

Palm Company

Sea Company and Sand Company

8-66. Since the management of the parent corporation, Palm Company, controls the activities of Sea Company and Sand Company, these three companies function as a single entity. The e __ __ __ __ __ concept requires that a set of financial statements be prepared for this family.

entity

8-67. Each corporation is a legal entity, with its own financial statements. The set of financial statements for the whole family brings together, or **consolidates,** these separate statements. The set for the whole family is therefore called a c __ __ __ __ __ __ __ __ __ __ __ d financial statement.

consolidated

8-68. For example, if Palm Company has $10,000 cash, Sea Company has $5,000 cash, and Sand Company has $4,000 cash, the whole family has $_____ cash, and this amount would be reported on the c_____ balance sheet.

$19,000

consolidated

8-69. An entity earns income by making sales to outside customers. It cannot earn income by dealing with itself. Corporations in the consolidated family may buy from and sell to one another. Transactions between members of the family . . . [do / do not] earn income for the consolidated entity. The effect of these **intrafamily transactions,** therefore, must be eliminated from the consolidated statements.

do not

3-36a. "Inventory costing $600 was purchased for cash." There was a decrease in Cash; so there was a . . . [debit / credit] to Cash. The other entry must be a . . . [debit / credit]. It was a . . . [debit / credit] to Inventory; it was an increase in that asset account.

credit

debit   debit

3-36b. "Inventory costing $400 was purchased on credit." There was an increase in Inventory, which is an asset, as is Cash, so there was a . . . [debit / credit] to Inventory. The other entry must be a . . . [debit / credit]. It was a . . . [debit / credit] to Accounts Payable; it was an increase in that liability account.

debit   credit

credit

3-36c. "Green Company paid $300 to a creditor." There was a decrease in Cash; so there was a . . . [debit / credit] to Cash. The other entry must be a . . . [debit / credit]. It was a . . . [debit / credit] to Accounts Payable; it was a decrease in that liability account.

credit

debit   debit

3-36d. "Green Company received $500 in cash from a credit customer." There was an increase in Cash; so there was a . . . [debit / credit] to Cash. The other entry must be a . . . [debit / credit]. It was a . . . [debit / credit] to Accounts Receivable; it was a decrease in that asset account.

debit

credit   credit

NOTE: Notice that after each transaction where the debits equal the credits, the fundamental accounting equation remains: Assets = Liabilities + Equity. Therefore, the balance sheet is always in balance.

DEBT RATIO

8-62. A common way of measuring the relative amount of debt and equity capital is the **debt ratio,** which is the ratio of debt capital to total permanent capital. Recall that **debt capital** is another name for . . . [total / current / noncurrent] liabilities. Equity capital consists of total Paid-in Capital plus R _ _ _ _ _ _ _ E _ _ _ _ _ _ _ _ .

noncurrent

Retained Earnings

8-63. Earlier you worked with the following permanent capital structure:

LOUGEE COMPANY

Sources and Uses of Permanent Capital
as of December 31, 2001

Uses of Capital		Sources of Capital	
Working capital	$ 6,000	Noncurrent liabilities	$ 9,000
Noncurrent assets	20,000	Equity	17,000
Total uses	$26,000	Total sources	$26,000

Calculate the debt ratio for Lougee Company.

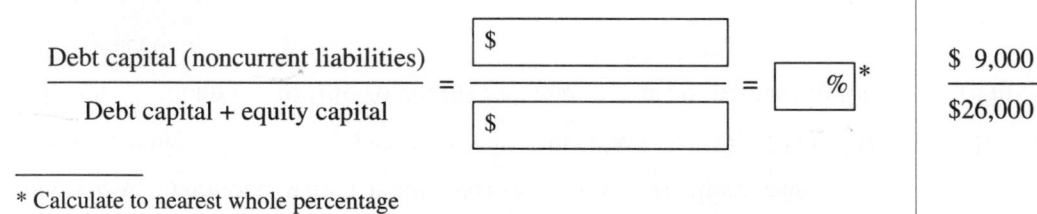

$$\frac{\text{Debt capital (noncurrent liabilities)}}{\text{Debt capital + equity capital}} = \frac{\$ \underline{\hphantom{xxxxxx}}}{\$ \underline{\hphantom{xxxxxx}}} = \boxed{\hphantom{xx}\%}^*$$

$\dfrac{\$\ 9,000}{\$26,000} = 35\%$

* Calculate to nearest whole percentage

8-64. Most industrial companies have a debt ratio of less than 50%. Lougee Company . . . [is / is not] in this category.

is

> **NOTE:** If one corporation owns more than 50% of the stock in another corporation, it can control the affairs of that corporation because it can outvote all other owners. Many businesses consist of a number of corporations that are legally separate entities but, because they are controlled by one corporation, are part of a single "family."

3-37. Because the total of the debit entries for any transaction should always equal the total of the credit entries, it is . . . [difficult / easy] to check the accuracy with which bookkeeping is done. (We owe this ingenious arrangement to Venetian merchants, who invented it more than 500 years ago.)

easy

INCOME STATEMENT ACCOUNTS

3-38. The accounts in Exhibit 3 were for items that appear on the balance sheet. Accounts are also kept for items that appear on another financial statement, the i n c o m e statement. As we saw in Part 2, this statement reports the revenues and the expenses of an accounting period and the difference between them, which is net i n c o m e .

income

income

> **NOTE:** In Part 2, we referred to the increase in Retained Earnings as "Income." From here on, we shall use the technically correct name: "Net Income." Net Income is the bottom line of the income statement. Various subtotals of income, such as Gross Income and Operating Income, are used in practice.

3-39. Revenues are . . . [increases / decreases] in equity during a period, and expenses are . . . [increases / decreases] in equity.

increases

decreases

3-40. For equity accounts, increases are recorded as . . . [debits / credits]. Because revenues are increases in equity, revenues are recorded as . . . [debits / credits].

credits

credits

3-41. Similarly, decreases in equity are recorded as . . . [debits / credits]. Because expenses are decreases in equity, expenses are recorded as . . . [debits / credits].

debits

debits

8-59. A company runs the risk of going bankrupt if it has too high a pro- | debt
portion of . . . [debt / equity] capital. A company pays an unnecessarily
high cost for its permanent capital if it has too high a proportion of . . .
[debt / equity] capital. | equity

8-60. A company that obtains a high proportion of its permanent capital
from debt is said to be **highly leveraged.** If such a company does not get
into financial difficulty, it will earn a high return for its equity investors
because each dollar of debt capital takes the place of a . . . [more / less] | more
expensive dollar of equity capital.

8-61. However, highly leveraged companies are risky because the high
proportion of debt capital and the associated requirement to pay interest
. . . [increases / decreases] the chance that the company will not be able | increases
to meet its obligations.

NOTE: In this introductory treatment, we focus on the basic differences between common stock and bonds. Some additional points are worth noting:

1. The interest on bonds is a tax-deductible expense to the corporation. If the annual interest expense on a 9% bond is $90,000, the corporation's taxable income is reduced by $90,000. At a tax rate of 40%, this means that the net cost to the corporation is only 60% of $90,000, or $54,000; the effective interest cost is 5.4%.

2. Preferred stock has risk and cost characteristics that are in between common stocks and bonds. Although dividends on preferred stock do not reduce a corporation's taxable income, many companies still use preferred stock as a source of capital.

3. In recent years, there has been a tremendous increase in the types of debt and equity securities. New financial instruments are structures with risk and cost characteristics designed to meet the needs of various types of investors.

3-42. The complete set of rules for making entries to accounts is as follows:

Increases in assets are [debits / credits].   debits

Decreases in assets are [debits / credits].   credits

Increases in liabilities and equity are [debits / credits].   credits

Decreases in liabilities and equity are [debits / credits].   debits

Increases in revenues are [debits / credits].   credits

Increases in expenses are [debits / credits].   debits

> **NOTE:** It is important that you learn these rules; they govern all accounting transactions. Also, although this may seem strange, it is a fact that both increases in assets (which are good things) and increases in expenses (which are not so good) are debits. That's the way it has to be, in order to maintain the basic equation.

THE LEDGER AND THE JOURNAL

3-43. A group of accounts, such as those for Green Company in Exhibit 3, is called a ledger. There is no standard form, so long as there is space to record the d r _ _ _ _ s and c r _ _ _ _ _ s to each account.   debits   credits
Exhibit 5 is the ___ledger___ of Glendale Market, the same company   ledger
we examined in Part 2.

3-44. In practice, transactions are not recorded directly in the ledger. First, they are written in a record such as Exhibit 4. The title of Exhibit 4 shows that this record is called a _____. The record made for   journal
each transaction is called a _____ entry.   journal

3-45. As Exhibit 4 shows, for each journal entry, the account to be . . . [debited / credited] is listed first, and the . . . [Dr. / Cr.] amount is entered   debited   Dr.
in the first of the two money columns. The account to be . . . [debited /   credited
credited] is listed below, and is indented. The . . . [Dr. / Cr.] amount is en-   Cr.
tered in the second money column.

8-54. Bonds are an obligation of the company that issues them, but stocks are not an obligation. Therefore, *investors* usually have more risk if they invest in a company's stock than if they invest in the bonds of the same company. They are not certain to get either dividends or repayment of their investment. Investors therefore demand a . . . [higher / lower] return from an investment in stock than from an investment in bonds in the same company.

higher *(The tradeoff between risk and return is a more advanced concept. It is beyond the scope of this introductory text.)*

8-55. For example, if a company's bonds had an interest rate of 7%, investors would invest in its stock only if they expected that the return on stock would be . . . [at least 7% / considerably more than 7%]. (The expected return on stock consists of both expected dividends and an expected increase in the market value of the stock.)

considerably more than 7%

8-56. Thus, from the viewpoint of the issuing company, stock, which is . . . [debt / equity] capital, is a . . . [more / less] expensive source of capital than bonds, which are . . . [debt / equity] capital.

equity   more
debt

8-57. Circle the correct words in the following table, which shows the principal differences between debt capital and equity capital.

	Bonds (Debt)	Stock (Equity)		
Annual payments required	[Yes / No]	[Yes / No]	Yes	No
Principal payments required	[Yes / No]	[Yes / No]	Yes	No
Risk to the entity is	[High / Low]	[High / Low]	High	Low
But its cost is relatively	[High / Low]	[High / Low]	Low	High

8-58. In deciding on its permanent capital structure, a company must decide on the proper balance between debt capital, which has a relatively . . . [high / low] risk and a relatively . . . [high / low] cost, and equity capital, which has a relatively . . . [high / low] risk and a relatively . . . [high / low] cost.

high   low
low   high

3-46. On January 8, merchandise costing $600 was sold for $900, and the customer agreed to pay $900 within 30 days. Using the two journal entries for January 7 as a guide, record the two parts of this transaction in the journal. (If you are not sure about how to record this transaction, go to Frame 3-47.)

8	Accounts Receivable	900	
	Revenues		900
8	Expenses	600	
	Inventory		600

(If you did this correctly, jump ahead to Frame 3-49.)

3-47. On January 8, merchandise costing $600 was sold for $900, and the customer agreed to pay $900 within 30 days.

The first part of this transaction is that the business earned **Revenues** of $900, and an asset, **Accounts Receivable,** increased by $900. Record this part of the transaction by completing the blanks below.

Dr. 900

Cr. 900

Dr. Accounts Receivable 900

Cr.   Revenues 900

> **HINT:** If you are uncertain as to whether a particular account is to be debited or credited, you usually can find out by referring to the other account in the entry. For example, the entry to Accounts Receivable is an increase in an asset, which is a debit, so the entry to Revenues must be a credit.

3-48. On January 8, merchandise costing $600 was sold for $900, and the customer agreed to pay $900 within 30 days.

The other part of this transaction is that the business had an **Expense** of $600 because its **Inventory** was decreased by $600. Record this part of the transaction by completing the blanks below.

Dr. 600

Cr. 600

Dr. Expenses 600

Cr.   Inventory 600

8-49. A stock split has the same effect as a stock dividend. Cash . . . [increases / decreases / is unchanged]. Retained Earnings . . . [increases / decreases / is unchanged]. The market price per share . . . [increases / decreases / is unchanged].

is unchanged	is unchanged
decreases	

> **NOTE:** Although arithmetically a "two-for-one" stock split cuts the market price in half, in practice the decrease might be slightly less than this. The reason is that stocks with moderate stock prices tend to be regarded more favorably by investors than stocks with very high prices. This is generally the principal reason for making a stock split.

BALANCE BETWEEN DEBT AND EQUITY CAPITAL

8-50. A corporation obtains some capital from retained earnings. In addition, it obtains capital from the issuance of stock, which is . . . [debt / equity] capital, and from the issuance of bonds, which is . . . [debt / equity] capital.

equity

debt

8-51. A corporation has no fixed obligations to its common shareholders; that is, the company . . . [must / need not] declare dividends each year, and . . . [must / need not] repay the amount the shareholders have invested.

need not

need not

8-52. A company has two fixed obligations to its bondholders, however:

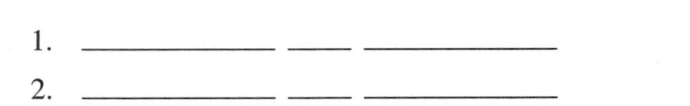

1. _____ ___ _____
2. _____ ___ _____

Payment of interest

Repayment of principal
(See Frame 8-12.)

8-53. If the company fails to pay either the interest or the principal when due, the bondholders may force the company into bankruptcy.

Evidently bonds are a . . . [less / more] risky method of raising capital by the corporation than stock; that is, debt capital is a . . . [less / more] risky source of capital than equity capital.

more

more

3-49. Journal entries are transferred to the l _ _ _ _ _ (as in Exhibit 5). This process is called **posting.** The entries through January 7 have already been posted to the ledger, as indicated by the check mark opposite each one. Post the journal entries for January 8 to the proper ledger accounts in Exhibit 5, and make check marks to show that you have posted them.

ledger

Accounts Receivable		Revenues	
900			300
			800
			900

Inventory		Expenses	
2,000	200	200	
2,000	500	500	
	600	*600*	

3-50. To summarize, any transaction requires at least (how many?) _____ changes in the accounts. These changes are recorded first in the . . . [ledger / journal]. They are then posted to the . . . [ledger / journal].

two

journal   ledger

THE CLOSING PROCESS

3-51. The Revenues account in Exhibit 5 reports . . . [increases / decreases] in Retained Earnings during the period, and the Expenses account reports . . . [increases / decreases] in Retained Earnings. As we know, the difference between revenues and expenses is the net i _ _ _ _ _ _ of the period.

increases

decreases

income

3-52. The net income for the period is an increase in the equity account, R _ _ _ _ _ _ _ _ _ E _ _ _ _ _ _ _ _ _ . Net income is added to this account by a series of journal entries called **closing entries.**

Retained Earnings

3-53. In order to do this, we first must find the balance in the account that is to be closed. What is the balance in the Revenues account in Exhibit 5? $_____.

$2,000 (= $300 + $800 + $900)

DISTRIBUTIONS TO SHAREHOLDERS

8-45. Most corporations make an annual cash payment to their common shareholders. This is called a **dividend.** If Crowley Company declared and paid a dividend of $5 per share, and if it had 100,000 shares of common stock outstanding, the dividend would be $_____.

$500,000

The journal entry to record the effect of this distribution on Cash and Retained Earnings would be:

Dr. _____ _____ .... _____

Cr. _____ .... _____

Retained Earnings 500,000
Cash 500,000

8-46. A company may distribute to shareholders a noncash asset, such as shares of stock in other companies it owns or even one of its products. The effect of this distribution is a . . . [debit / credit] to Retained Earnings and an equal . . . [debit / credit] to the asset account.

debit
credit

8-47. Crowley Company might declare a **stock dividend.** If it distributed one share of its own stock for each 10 shares of stock outstanding, shareholders would have more shares. No asset decreased, so, in order to maintain equality, Equity would . . . [increase / decrease / be unchanged].

be unchanged

8-48. Similarly, Crowley might send its shareholders additional shares equal to the number of shares they own, or even double or triple this number of shares. Crowley may do this because it believes a high market price per share has an undesirable influence in trading the stock. This is called a **stock split.** If Crowley's stock previously had a market price of $200 per share for its 100,000 shares, and it made a "two-for-one" stock split, the number of shares of stock outstanding would . . . [increase / decrease / not change]. Cash would . . . [increase / decrease / not change]. The market price per share would . . . [increase / decrease / not change].

increase
not change
decrease

3-54. An entry is made that reduces the balance in the account to be closed to zero and records the same amount in the Retained Earnings account. Because the Revenues account has a . . . [Dr. / Cr.] balance, the entry that reduces Revenues to zero must be on the other side; that is, it must be a . . . [Dr. / Cr.].

Cr.

Dr.

3-55. In Exhibit 4, write the journal entry that closes the $2,000 balance in the Revenues account to the Retained Earnings account. (Date it January 8, the end of the accounting period.)

8   Revenues 2,000
        Retained Earnings   2,000

3-56. Using similar reasoning, write the journal entry that closes the $1,300 balance in the Expenses account to the Retained Earnings account.

8   Retained Earnings 1,300
        Expenses   1,300

3-57. Next, post these two entries to the ledger in Exhibit 5.

The accounts affected are:

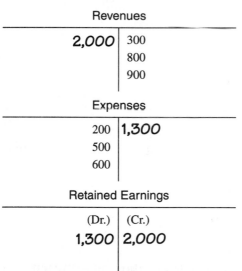

Revenues	
2,000	300
	800
	900

Expenses	
200	**1,300**
500	
600	

Retained Earnings	
(Dr.)	(Cr.)
1,300	**2,000**

8-40. The Retained Earnings account . . . [decreases / increases] by the amount of net income each period and . . . [decreases / increases] by the amount of dividends. Thus, if Retained Earnings are $100,000 at the start of a period during which a dividend of $20,000 is declared and during which net income is $30,000, Retained Earnings will be $_____ at the end of the period.

increases

decreases

$110,000
  (= $100,000 − $20,000 + $30,000)

8-41. Net income refers to the increase in equity . . . [in one year / over the life of the corporation to date], whereas **retained earnings** refers to the net increases, after deduction of dividends, . . . [in one year / over the life of the corporation to date].

in one year

over the life of the corporation to date

8-42. Retained earnings is one **source** of capital. It is reported on the . . . [left / right] side of the balance sheet. The capital is in the form of assets, and assets are reported on the . . . [left / right] side of the balance sheet.

right

left

> **NOTE:** Some people think that retained earnings are assets. Retained earnings are *not* assets. Remember that Cash is an asset. Therefore, retained earnings are *not* cash.

8-43. Equity is sometimes called "net worth." This term suggests that the amount of equity shows what the owners' claim on the assets is *worth*. Because the amounts reported on the assets side of the balance sheet . . . [do / do not] represent the real worth of these assets, this suggestion is . . . [approximately correct / dead wrong].

do not

dead wrong

8-44. The actual **worth** of a company's stock is what people will pay for it. This is the market price of the stock, which . . . [does / does not] appear anywhere on the balance sheet.

does not

3-58. To get ready for preparing the financial statements, the balance in each asset, liability, and equity account is calculated. (Revenue and expense accounts have zero balances because of the closing process.) For the Cash account in Exhibit 5, the calculation is as follows:

Cash

(Dr.)	(Cr.)
10,000	2,000
5,000	
300	
800	
16,100	**2,000**
Balance **14,100**	

> **NOTE:** Each side is totaled. A single line is drawn above the total. A double line is drawn beneath the total. The difference between the two totals is entered beneath the double line.

Calculate the balance for each account in Exhibit 5.

(Details are not shown here. The amounts can be checked against the amounts in Frame 3-60.)

3-59. Journal entries *change* the balance in the account. The *calculation* of the balance does not change the balance. Therefore the calculation of a balance . . . [does / does not] require a journal entry.

does not

3-60. The balance sheet is prepared from the balances in the asset, liability, and equity accounts. Complete the balance sheet for Glendale Market, as of January 8, in Exhibit 6.

GLENDALE MARKET
Balance Sheet as of January 8

Assets		Liabilities & Equity	
Cash	$14,100	Accounts payable	$ 2,000
Accounts receivable ..	900	Note payable	5,000
Inventory ..	2,700	Paid-in capital	10,000
		Retained earnings ...	700
Total Assets	$17,700	Total Liabilities and Equity	$17,700

PREFERRED STOCK

8-34. Some corporations issue stock that gives its owners preferential treatment over the common shareholders. As the word "preferential" suggests, such stock is called p __ __ __ __ __ __ ed stock.

preferred

8-35. Usually preferred shareholders have a preferential claim over the common shareholders for the par value of their stock. Thus, if the corporation were liquidated, the owner of 500 shares of $100 preferred stock would have to receive $_____ before the common shareholders received anything.

$50,000 (= 500 * $100)

8-36. As you learned earlier, par value of common stock has . . . [some / almost no] significance. Because preferred stock usually does have a preferential claim on assets equal to its par value, its par value has . . . [some / almost no] significance.

almost no

some

8-37. Preferred shareholders usually have rights to a stated amount of dividends. ADAPT Corporation has issued $100,000 of 9% preferred stock. No dividend can be paid to common shareholders until the preferred shareholders have received their full dividend of 9% of $100,000, amounting to $_____ per year.

$9,000

RETAINED EARNINGS AND DIVIDENDS

8-38. The net income of a period increases e __ __ __ __ __ . The directors may vote to distribute money to the shareholders in the form of **dividends.** Dividends decrease e __ __ __ __ __ .

equity

equity

8-39. Earnings is another name for "net income." If earnings are not distributed as dividends, they are **retained** in the corporation. This amount is reported on the balance sheet as R __ __ __ __ __ __ __ E __ __ __ __ __ __ s.

Retained
Earnings

3-61. The income statement is prepared from information in the Retained Earnings account. Complete the income statement in Exhibit 6.

Revenues	$2,000
Expenses	1,300
Net income	$ 700

3-62. After the closing process, the revenue and expense accounts have . . . [debit / credit / zero] balances. These accounts are therefore **temporary** accounts. They are started over at the beginning of each period. The asset accounts have . . . [debit / credit / zero] balances, and the liability and equity accounts have . . . [debit / credit / zero] balances; these balances are carried forward to the next period. Income statement accounts are . . . [temporary / permanent] accounts, and balance sheet accounts are . . . [temporary / permanent] accounts.

zero

debit
credit

temporary
permanent

3-63. Most entities report individual items of revenues and expenses (such as salary expense, maintenance expense, insurance expense) on their income statement. In order to do this, they set up an account for each item. Thus, if the income statement reported 2 revenue items and 10 expense items, there would be at least _____ (how many?) revenue and expense accounts. We shall describe these accounts in later Parts. The entries to them are made in exactly the same way as in the simple example given here.

12

3-64. Management needs more detailed information than is contained in the financial statements. For example, instead of one account, Accounts Receivable, it needs an account for each customer so that the amount owed by each customer is known. Therefore the ledger usually contains . . . [the same number of / many more] accounts than there are items on the financial statements.

many more

> **NOTE:** Although you need to understand the bookkeeping process described in this part, you don't need to memorize the details. Our purpose is to show where the numbers in the financial statements come from. This helps you understand what the numbers mean.

8-29. The balance sheet amount for common stock is the amount for the number of shares of stock outstanding.

Maxim Company has authorized 100,000 shares of stock. It has issued 60,000 shares, for which it received the stated value of $10 per share. As of December 31, 2001, it has bought back 10,000 shares, paying $10 per share. These shares are its treasury stock. The balance sheet amount for common stock is $_____.

$500,000 [= (60,000 * $10) − (10,000 * $10)]

8-30. Shareholders may sell their stock to other investors. Such sales . . . [do / do not] affect the balance sheet of the corporation. This is an example of the __ __ __ __ __ __ concept.

do not

entity

8-31. When shareholders sell their stock to other investors, the price at which the sale takes place is determined in the **marketplace.** The value at which a stock is sold in such a transaction is called the . . . [market / par / stated] value.

market

8-32. The market value of a company's stock has no necessary relation to its par value, its stated value, or the amount of paid-in capital. If the par value of a certain stock is $1, the market value . . . [will be $1 / can be any value].

can be any value

If the stated value of another stock is $10, the market value . . . [will be $10 / can be any value].

can be any value

If paid-in capital is $12 per share, the market value . . . [will be $12 / can be any value].

can be any value

8-33. The amount reported as total equity equals total assets less total liabilities. On the balance sheet, this is not likely to equal the total market value of all stock outstanding. Evidently accounting . . . [does / does not] report the market value of the shareholders' equity.

does not

A NOTE ON COMPUTERS

Most entities use a computer to do their accounting. The computer makes debit and credit entries according to exactly the same rules as those we have described. In this program, we must show the journal entries manually because what goes on inside the computer is not visible. The computer has the following advantages over the manual system we use in this program:

- The computer is much faster.

- The computer does not make copying errors. For example, when the computer writes a check, the amount of the check is always the amount credited to Cash and debited to some other account. The amounts reported on the financial statement are the same as the balances in the accounts.

- The computer ensures that debit entries always equal credit entries. It will not accept an entry in which this equality does not exist.

- Once an amount has been recorded in the computer, it may be used for several purposes. For example, an entry to Accounts Receivable is used in calculating the total amount in the Accounts Receivable account, the accounts of individual customers, and the amount reported on the balance sheet.

- The computer does not make arithmetic errors.

- The computer may require that certain rules be followed. For example, the credit entry for a check is always to the Cash account.

- The computer has built-in safeguards that help detect fraudulent or erroneous entries.

- In a company at several locations, an entry generated at one location can be transferred accurately to the central chart of accounts via the Internet. Companies have a chart of accounts that gives an account number for every possible transaction in the system. This can help to ensure the tracking of information if it is necessary.

However, if the initial input to the computer is made by a person, an error made by that person may not be detected. For example, if a check is supposed to be for $962 and the bookkeeper keys in $926, the computer may not detect the error. (Some input errors can be avoided by the use of automatic input devices, such as scanners that read bar codes.)

8-25. If Jones's payment of $10,000 was the only equity transaction, this section of the Marple Company balance sheet would appear as follows:

Common stock . . . . $_____		$ 1,000
Additional paid-in capital . . . . _____		9,000
		_____
Total paid-in capital . . . . $_____		$10,000

8-26. Not all stocks have a par value. For these **no-par-value stocks,** the directors **state** a value. This value, called the s __ __ __ __ d value, is usually set close to the amount that the corporation actually receives from the issuance of the stock. The difference between this amount and cash received is A __ __ __ __ __ __ __ __ __ P __ __ __ - __ __ C __ __ __ __ __ __ __ , just as in the case of par-value stock.

stated

Additional Paid-in Capital

8-27. When a corporation is formed, its directors vote to **authorize** a certain number of shares of stock and generally to **issue** some of this authorized stock to investors. Thus, at any given time the amount of stock authorized is usually . . . [larger than / the same as / smaller than] the amount issued.

larger than

8-28. A corporation may buy back some of the stock that it had previously issued. Such stock is called **treasury stock.** The **outstanding stock** consists of the issued stock less the treasury stock.

If a company issues 100,000 shares and buys back 15,000 shares, its treasury stock is _____ shares, and its outstanding stock is _____ shares.

15,000
85,000 (=100,000 − 15,000)

Also, despite the built-in safeguards, the computer cannot detect certain types of fraudulent entries. As examples of multimillion dollar errors reported in the press demonstrate, there is no guarantee that errors do not exist. Therefore, there must be an audit function to check the possibility of fraud or error.

Although the computer may perform most of the bookkeeping functions, it cannot replace the accountant. The accountant specifies the rules to be followed in routine transactions, but, as we shall see, some transactions require judgment about the accounts affected and the amounts to be debited or credited. The accountant must tell the computer how to make these entries. If the accountant makes an incorrect decision, the accounts will be incorrect.

Most important is the fact that learning the financial accounting transactions and closing processes as you are doing here cannot be replaced by a computer. It is basic to the understanding of the underlying processes. Once you understand the mechanics behind and structure of the financial statements, using a computer to facilitate their completion makes sense.

KEY POINTS TO REMEMBER

- **Debit** refers to the left side of an account and **credit** to the right side.

- Increases in asset and expense accounts are debits.

- Increases in liability, equity, and revenue accounts are credits.

- Decreases are the opposite.

- For any transaction, debits must equal credits. For the whole set of accounts, debit balances must equal credit balances.

- Transactions are first recorded in a journal. Amounts are then posted to the accounts in a ledger.

- Revenue and expense accounts are temporary accounts. At the end of each accounting period, they are closed to Retained Earnings. The difference between the revenues of a period and the expenses of the period is the net income of the period. These revenues and expenses are reported on the income statement.

- Net income is the increase in retained earnings from operating performance during the period.

- Asset, liability, and equity accounts are permanent accounts. Their balances are carried forward to the next accounting period.

COMMON STOCK

8-23. Some stock is issued with a specific amount printed on the face of each certificate. This amount is called the **par value.** In the stock certificate shown below, for example, the par value is $_____.

$.01
(See the upper right-hand corner.)

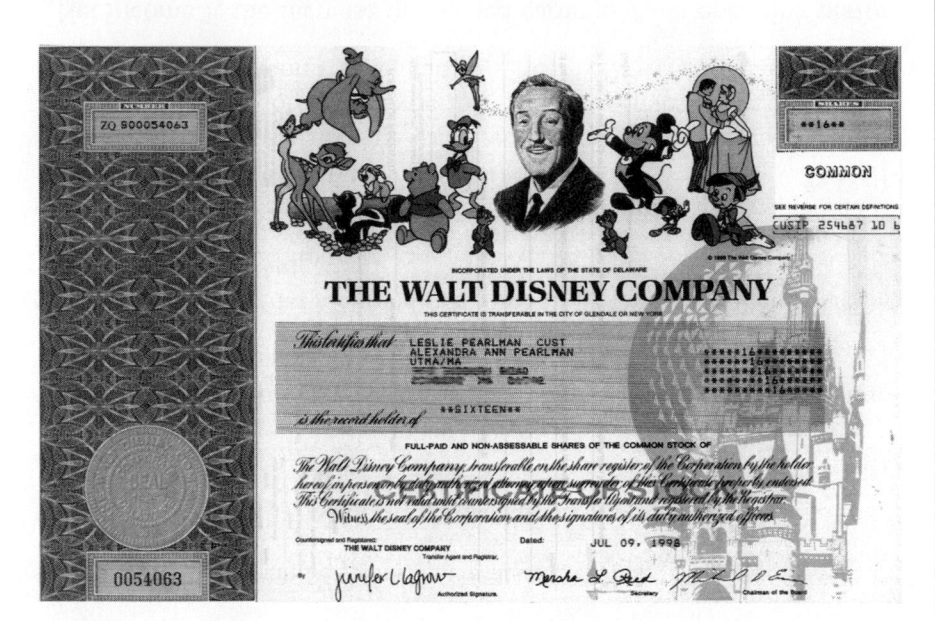

NOTE: Strangely, the par value of stock has almost no significance. It is a holdover from the days when shareholders were liable if they purchased stock for less than its par value. In order to avoid this liability, stock today is almost always issued for much more than its par value. Nevertheless, the par value of stock continues to be reported on the balance sheet, often accompanied by a notation.

8-24. The amount that the shareholders paid the corporation in exchange for their stock is **paid-in capital.** The difference between par value and the total paid-in capital is called **additional paid-in capital.**

Jones paid $10,000 cash to Marple Company and received 1,000 shares of its $1 par-value common stock. Complete the journal entry that Marple Company would make for this transaction.

Dr. Cash . . . . _____	10,000
Cr. Common stock . . . . _____	1,000 (at par value)
Cr. Additional paid-in capital . . . . _____	9,000

You have completed Part 3 of this program. If you think you understand the material in this part, you should now take Post Test 3, which is in the separate booklet. If you are uncertain about your understanding, you should review Part 3.

The post test will serve both to test your comprehension and to review the highlights of Part 3. After taking the post test, you may find that you are unsure about certain points. You should review these points before going on to Part 4.

8-19. A **partnership** is an unincorporated business owned by two or more persons jointly. If there are only a few partners, the equity of each would be shown separately.

John Black and Henry Brown are equal partners in a laundry business. On December 31, 2001, the equity in the business totaled $100,000. The equity might be reported on that date as follows:

_____ _____, Capital	$_____	John Black, Capital	$ 50,000
_____ _____, Capital	_____	Henry Brown, Capital	50,000
Total equity	$_____	Total equity	$100,000

8-20. Equity in a partnership consists of capital paid in by owners plus earnings retained in the business. Thus the item "John Black, Capital, $50,000" means (circle the correct answer):

   A. John Black contributed $50,000 cash to the entity.

   B. The entity owes John Black $50,000.

   C. John Black's ownership interest in the assets is $50,000.

C

Not A: We don't know the amount of the original contribution.

Not B: Unlike its bondholders, the entity does not "owe" its owners.

8-21. Owners of a **corporation** are called **shareholders** because they hold shares of the corporation's stock. The equity section of a corporation's balance sheet is therefore labeled s _ _ _ _ _ _ _ _ _ _

e _ _ _ _ y.

shareholder

equity

8-22. There are two types of shareholders: **common shareholders** and **preferred shareholders.** The stock held by the former is called _____ stock, and that held by the latter is called _____ stock. We shall first describe accounting for common stock.

common

preferred

> **NOTE:** Most organizations are proprietorships, partnerships, or corporations. Other forms, not described here, include limited partnerships, trusts, and S Corporations. Special rules apply to equity transactions and/or tax accounting in these organizations.

Part 4

Revenues and Monetary Assets

Learning Objectives

In this part you will learn:

- The accounting period.
- What accrual accounting is.
- Three more of the nine basic accounting concepts:
    - Conservatism concept.
    - Materiality concept.
    - Realization concept.
- How revenue items are measured.
- How monetary assets are measured.
- The days' sales uncollected ratio.

4-1. In Part 3 we introduced the idea of Net Income, which is the difference between r _ _ _ _ _ _ _ _ and e _ _ _ _ _ _ _ _ .

revenues expenses

4-2. Net Income increases Retained Earnings. Retained Earnings is an item of . . . [liabilities / equity] on the balance sheet. Any increase in Retained Earnings is also an increase in . . . [liabilities / equity].

equity

equity

> **NOTE:** Net income results from the profitable operation of an entity. The amount of net income is one of the most important items of information that accounting reports. In this part we describe how the revenue portion of net income is measured.

8-16. Some companies obtain funds by issuing an instrument that is backed by other instruments. For example, a bank may issue an instrument that promises to pay interest from a portfolio of mortgages it holds. The return on such an instrument is derived from the underlying mortgages, and the instrument is therefore called a d __ __ __ __ __ __ ive.

derivative

> **NOTE:** Derivatives may be backed by a complicated set of promises. Therefore, measuring the value of a derivative and accounting for this value may be extremely complicated. Accounting for derivatives is described in advanced texts.

TYPES OF EQUITY CAPITAL

8-17. As noted in earlier parts, there are two sources of equity capital:

1. Amounts paid in by equity investors, who are the entity's owners. This amount is called . . . [Paid-in Capital / Retained Earnings].

Paid-in Capital

2. Amounts generated by the profitable operation of the entity. This amount is called . . . [Paid-in Capital / Retained Earnings].

Retained Earnings

8-18. Some entities do not report these two sources separately. An unincorporated business owned by a single person is called a **proprietorship.** The equity item in a proprietorship is often reported by giving the proprietor's name, followed by the word "Capital."

Mary Green is the proprietor of Green's Market. Green's Market has total equity of $10,000. Show how the owner's equity item would look by filling in the blanks.

Mary Green, _____ . . . . $_____

Capital $10,000

FISCAL YEAR

4-3. An income statement reports the amount of net income . . . [at a moment in time / over a period of time]. The period of time covered by one income statement is called the **accounting period.**

over a period of time

4-4. For most entities, the official accounting period is one year, referred to as the **fiscal year.** However, financial statements, called **interim statements,** usually are prepared for shorter periods. In Part 3 you prepared an income statement for Glendale Market for the period January 2 through January 8. This was an . . . [annual / interim] statement, and the accounting period was one . . . [week / month / year].

interim
week

4-5. Entities don't fire their employees and cease operations at the end of an accounting period. They continue from one accounting period to the next. The fact that accounting divides the stream of events into f _ _ _ _ _ y _ _ _ s makes the problem of measuring revenues and expenses in a fiscal year . . . [an easy / the most difficult] problem in accounting.

fiscal years
the most difficult

ACCRUAL ACCOUNTING

4-6. On January 3, Glendale Market borrowed $5,000 from a bank. Its cash therefore . . . [increased / decreased / did not change]. A liability . . . [increased / decreased / did not change].

increased
increased

4-7. Revenues are increases in equity. The receipt of $5,000 cash as a loan from the bank on January 3 . . . [increased / decreased / did not change] Glendale Market revenues and therefore . . . [increased / decreased / did not change] equity.

did not change
did not change

4-8. On January 4, Glendale Market purchased $2,000 of inventory, paying cash. This was an increase in one asset and a decrease in another asset. Since equity was unchanged, the payment of cash on January 4 . . . [was / was not] associated with an expense.

was not

8-12. When an entity issues bonds, it assumes two obligations: (1) to repay the face amount, the **principal,** on the due date, and (2) to pay **interest,** often, but not always, at semiannual intervals (i.e., twice a year). The obligation to pay the principal is usually a . . . [current / noncurrent] liability. The liability for interest that has been earned but is unpaid is a . . . [current / noncurrent] liability.

noncurrent

current

8-13. Interest on bonds is an expense and should be recognized in the accounting period to which the interest applies. Thus, if in January 2002 an entity makes a semiannual interest payment of $3,000 to cover the last six months of 2001, this interest expense should be recognized in 20 __ __ . This is required by the m __ __ __ __ __ __ __ g concept.

2001   matching

8-14. The $3,000 of unpaid interest that was an expense in 2001 is recorded in 2001 by the following entry:

Dr. I _____ E _____ 3,000

    Cr. I _____ P _____ 3,000

Interest Expense

  Interest Payable

8-15. In 2002, when this interest was paid to the bondholders, the following entry would be made:

Dr. _____ _____ 3,000

    Cr. _____ 3,000

Interest Payable 3,000

  Cash 3,000

As the above entries indicate, on the balance sheet, at any given time, the liability for the principal payment is the total face value of the bond, but the interest liability is the . . . [amount of interest expense incurred but unpaid / total amount of interest].

amount of interest expense incurred but unpaid

4-9. On January 8, Glendale Market sold merchandise for $900, and the customer agreed to pay $900 within 30 days. This transaction resulted in . . . [an increase / a decrease / no change] in cash. Revenue was $_____. This revenue . . . [was / was not] associated with a change in cash on January 8.

no change

$900   was not

4-10. Evidently revenues and expenses . . . [are / are not] always accompanied, at the same time, by changes in cash. Moreover, changes in cash . . . [are / are not] always coupled with corresponding changes in revenues or expenses.

are not

are not

4-11. Increases or decreases in cash are changes in an . . . [equity / asset] account. Revenues or expenses are changes in an . . . [equity / asset] account.

asset

equity

4-12. Net income is measured as the difference between . . . [cash increases and cash decreases / revenues and expenses].

revenues and expenses

4-13. Net income measures the increase in e __ __ __ __ __ during an accounting period that was associated with earnings activities.

equity

4-14. Many individuals and some small businesses keep track only of cash receipts and cash payments. This type of accounting is called c __ __ __ accounting. If you keep a record of your bank deposits, the checks you write, and the balance in your bank account, you are doing __ __ __ __ accounting. Cash accounting . . . [does / does not] measure changes in equity.

cash

cash   does not

8-8. A common source of debt capital is the issuance of **bonds.** A bond is a written promise to pay someone who lends money to the entity. Since a bond usually is a noncurrent liability, the payments are due . . . [within one year / sometime after one year].

sometime after one year

8-9. The total amount that must be repaid is specified on the face of a bond and is termed the **face amount.**

If Green Company issues 10-year bonds whose face amounts total $100,000, Green Company has a liability, Bonds Payable, of $_____.

$100,000

> **NOTE:** If the entity does not receive cash equal to the face amount of the bonds in connection with their issuance, there are accounting complications not discussed in this introductory program.

8-10. Suppose that Green Company receives $100,000 cash from the issuance of bonds that have a face amount of $100,000. Write the journal entry necessary to record the effect of this transaction on the Cash and Bonds Payable accounts.

Dr. _____ . . . . _____

Cr. _____ _____ . . . . _____

Cash 100,000

Bonds Payable 100,000

8-11. When they are issued, the bonds are . . . [current / noncurrent] liabilities. However, as time passes and the due date becomes less than one year, a bond becomes a . . . [current / noncurrent] liability. In 2001, a bond that is due on January 1, 2003, would be a . . . [current / noncurrent] liability. In 2002, the same bond would be a . . . [current / noncurrent] liability.

noncurrent

current
noncurrent
current

4-15. Most entities, however, account for revenues and expenses, as well as for cash receipts and cash payments. This type of accounting is called **accrual accounting.** Evidently, accrual accounting is . . . [simpler / more complicated] than cash accounting, but accrual accounting . . . [does / does not] measure changes in equity. The most difficult problems in accounting are problems of . . . [cash / accrual] accounting.

more complicated
does

accrual

4-16. Because net income is the change in equity and measures the entity's financial performance, accrual accounting provides . . . [more / less] information than cash accounting.

more

4-17. In order to measure the net income of a period, we must measure
r __ __ __ __ __ __ s and e __ __ __ __ __ __ s of that period, and this
requires the use of __ __ __ __ __ __ __ accounting.

revenues   expenses
accrual

CONSERVATISM CONCEPT

> **NOTE:** In this part, we describe the measurement of revenues. The measurement of expenses is described in later parts. First, we shall introduce three more accounting concepts: conservatism, materiality, and realization.

4-18. Suppose that in January, Lynn Jones agreed to buy an automobile from Ace Auto Company; the automobile is to be delivered to Jones in March. Because Ace Auto Company is in the business of selling automobiles, it . . . [would / would not] be happy that Jones has agreed to buy one.

would

4-19. Jones agreed in January to buy an automobile for delivery in March. Although Jones is . . . [likely / unlikely] to take delivery in March, it is possible that she will change her mind. The sale of this automobile therefore is . . . [absolutely certain / uncertain].

likely

uncertain

SOURCES OF CAPITAL

8-5. To highlight how working capital and the noncurrent assets were financed, we can rearrange the items on the balance sheet as follows:

LOUGEE COMPANY
Sources and Uses of Permanent Capital
as of December 31, 2001

Uses of Capital		Sources of Capital	
	$ 6,000	Noncurrent liabilities	$ 9,000
Noncurrent assets	20,000	Equity	17,000
Total uses	$26,000	Total sources	$26,000

Fill in the box above.

Working capital

8-6. The right-hand side of the balance sheet given above shows the sources of capital used to finance the working capital and the noncurrent assets. Collectively, these sources are called **permanent capital.** As the balance sheet indicates, there are two sources of permanent capital:

(1) N __ __ __ __ __ __ __ __ t l __ __ __ __ __ __ __ __ __ __ __ s, and
(2) E __ __ __ __ y. The total of these two sources is $_____, and they are used to finance assets that also total $_____ .

Noncurrent liabilities

Equity $26,000

$26,000

> **NOTE:** In this part we describe the two types of permanent capital and how they are recorded in the accounts. Although these items are often called "capital," they are more accurately labeled "sources of capital."

DEBT CAPITAL

8-7. Although most liabilities are debts, the term **debt capital** refers only to noncurrent liabilities. Debt capital therefore refers to liabilities that come due . . . [within one year / sometime after one year].

sometime after one year

4-20. Jones agreed in January to buy an automobile for delivery in March.

Because in January the sale of this automobile is uncertain, accounting . . . [does / does not] recognize the revenue in January. If Jones does accept delivery in March, accounting recognizes r __ __ __ __ __ __ in March. This is a . . . [conservative / liberal] way to account for the transaction.

does not

revenue

conservative

4-21. Increases in equity are recognized only when they are **reasonably certain.** To be conservative, decreases in equity should be recognized as soon as they probably occurred. Suppose an automobile was stolen from Ace Auto Company in January, and the company waits until March to decide that the automobile is gone for good. Conservatism requires that the decrease in equity be recognized when it is **reasonably possible;** that is, in . . . [January / March].

January

4-22. The conservatism concept therefore has two parts:

1. Recognize **increases** in equity only when they are reasonably . . . [certain / possible].

   certain

2. Recognize **decreases** in equity as soon as they are reasonably . . . [certain / possible].

   possible

> **NOTE:** These are general ideas only. Specifics will be given in later parts of this program.

MATERIALITY CONCEPT

4-23. A brand new pencil is a(n) . . . [asset / liability / equity] of the entity that owns it.

asset

4-24. Every time an employee writes with a pencil, part of the asset's value . . . [increases / decreases], and the entity's equity also . . . [increases / decreases].

decreases   decreases

LOUGEE COMPANY

Balance Sheet as of December 31, 2001

	[ ]		[ ]	and [ ]	
Current	[ ]	$10,000	Current	[ ]	$ 4,000
Noncurrent	[ ]	20,000	Noncurrent	[ ]	9,000
			Paid-in capital		7,000
			Retained earnings		10,000
				[ ]	
Total	[ ]	$30,000	Total		$30,000

Assets   Liabilities and Equity

assets   liabilities

assets   liabilities

Assets   Liabilities and Equity

8-2. Current assets are assets that are expected to be turned into cash within _____ _____ (what period of time?). Current liabilities are obligations that come due within _____ _____ (what period of time?).

one year

one

year

8-3. For Lougee Company, we can say that $4,000 of the $10,000 in current assets was financed by the c __ __ __ __ __ __ __ liabilities. The remaining $6,000 of current assets and the $20,000 of noncurrent assets were financed by the $9,000 of _____ _____ plus the $17,000 of _____.

current

noncurrent liabilities

equity

8-4. That part of the current assets not financed by the current liabilities is called **working capital.** Working capital is therefore the difference between c _____ a _____ and c _____ l _____. In the example given above, working capital is:

$_____ − $_____ = $_____.

current assets   current

liabilities

$10,000 − $4,000 = $6,000

4-25. Would it be possible, theoretically, to find out each day the number of partly used pencils and to make a journal entry showing the amount of pencils that were used up and the corresponding "pencil expense" of that day? . . . [Yes / No] Would it be practical? . . . [Yes / No]

Yes   No

4-26. The accountant considers that the asset value of pencils was entirely used up at the time they were issued to the user. To do otherwise would be a waste of time. This solution is simple and . . . [impractical / practical], but . . . [more / less] exact than the theoretically correct treatment.

practical

less

4-27. The treatment of pencils is an example of the **materiality** concept. The materiality concept states that the accountant may disregard im __ __ __ __ __ __ __ __ events. When accountants consider the asset value of pencils to be entirely used up when they are issued to the user, they are applying the __ __ __ __ __ __ __ __ __ __ __ __ concept.

immaterial

materiality

> **NOTE:** Material transactions are those that make a difference in understanding an entity's financial affairs. Deciding which transactions are material is a matter of judgment. There are no mechanical rules.

4-28. The other side of the coin is that the financial statements must disclose all material facts. For example, if a large fraction of a company's inventory is found to be worthless, the m _____ concept requires that this fact be recorded in the accounts.

materiality

4-29. The materiality concept therefore has two parts: (1) . . . [disregard / disclose] trivial (i.e., unimportant) matters, and (2) . . . [disregard / disclose] all important matters.

disregard

disclose

Part 8

Liabilities and Equity

Learning Objectives

In this part, you will learn:

- The nature of working capital.
- Types of permanent capital: debt and equity.
- How to account for debt capital.
- Accounting for equity capital in Proprietorships, Partnerships, and Corporations.
    - Paid-in capital: common and preferred stock.
    - Retained earnings and dividends.
- The debt / equity ratio.
- The nature of consolidated financial statements.

WORKING CAPITAL

8-1. In earlier parts you learned that the balance sheet has two sides with equal totals. Fill in the two missing names in the boxes in the simplified balance sheet given on the following page.

4-30. To review, the conservatism concept is this: recognize increases in equity only when they are r __ __ __ __ __ __ __ __ __ c __ __ __ __ __ __ , but recognize decreases as soon as they are r __ __ __ __ __ __ __ __ __ __ p __ __ __ __ __ __ __ . The materiality concept is this: . . . [disregard / disclose] trivial matters, but . . . [disregard / disclose] all important matters.

REALIZATION CONCEPT

4-31. Consider an entity that manufactures goods and then sells them. In accounting, the revenue from these goods is recognized at the time they are delivered to the customer, *not* at the time they are manufactured.

Morgan Company manufactured an item in February, delivered it to a customer in March, and the customer paid for it in April. Revenue should be recognized in . . . [February / March / April].

March

February	March	April
Goods manufactured	Goods delivered	Cash received

Revenue recognized

4-32. If a company sells services rather than goods, revenue is recognized at the time the services are . . . [contracted for / delivered].

delivered

4-33. Goods (such as shoes) are *tangible* products. Services (such as repairing computers) are *intangible* products. Both goods and services are products. Thus, the general rule is that revenue from a product is recognized when the product is . . . [manufactured / contracted for / delivered].

delivered

4-34. At the time of delivery, revenue is said to be realized. The realization concept is that revenue is recognized and recorded in the period in which it is r __ __ __ __ __ ed.

realized

The post test will serve both to test your comprehension and to review the highlights of Part 7. After taking the post test, you may find that you are unsure about certain points. You should review these points before going on to Part 8.

4-35. In January, Smith Company contracts to paint Herbert's house. The house is painted in February, and Herbert pays Smith Company in March. Smith Company should recognize revenue in _____ (what month?).

February

January	February	March
Services ordered	Services delivered	Cash received

Revenue
recognized

4-36. Gordon Company manufactures some imitation carrots in May. In June it receives an order from Peter Rabbit, Esq., for one carrot. Gordon Company delivers the carrot in July. Peter Rabbit pays the bill in August and eats the carrot in September. Gordon Company would recognize revenue in _____, which is . . . [before / after] the order was received and . . . [before / after] the cash was received.

July   after
before

4-37. Revenue is realized when a *sale* is completed by the delivery of a product. Because of this, the word "sales" is often used along with revenue, as in the phrase "s _____ r _____."

sales revenue

4-38. A salesperson may say that he or she has "made a sale" when the order was written, even though the product is to be delivered at some future time. In accounting, writing a sales order . . . [is / is not] a sale because the revenue has not yet been __ __ __ __ __ __ ed.

is not
realized

NOTE: Revenue may be recognized (1) before, (2) during, or (3) after the period in which the cash from the sale is received. First, consider a case in which revenue is recognized in the same period as when the cash is received.

4-39. In January, Loren Company sold and delivered a motorcycle to Jerry Paynter, who paid $1,800 cash.

In this example, revenue is recognized in the . . . [month before / same month as / month after] the related cash receipt.

same month as

KEY POINTS TO REMEMBER

- When acquired, a plant asset is recorded at its cost, including installation and other costs of making the asset ready for its intended use.

- Land has an unlimited life and is rarely depreciated.

- Plant assets are depreciated over their service life. Each year, a fraction of their cost is debited to Depreciation Expense and credited to Accumulated Depreciation.

- Depreciation Expense is an estimate. We do not know how long the service life will be, nor the asset's residual value.

- The book value of a plant asset is the difference between its cost and its accumulated depreciation. When book value reaches zero or the residual value, no more depreciation expense is recorded.

- Book value does *not* report what the asset is worth.

- When an asset is sold, the difference between the sale price and book value is a gain or loss and is so reported on the income statement.

- In financial accounting, depreciation is calculated either by an accelerated method or by the straight-line method.

- In the units-of-production method, the annual depreciation expense is calculated by multiplying the number of service units produced in that year by a unit cost. This unit cost is found by dividing the asset's depreciable cost by the number of service units estimated to be produced over the asset's total life.

- In the straight-line method, the annual depreciation expense is calculated by multiplying the asset's depreciable cost by a constant percentage. This percentage is found by dividing 1 by the number of years in the asset's estimated service life.

- Accelerated depreciation is often used for income tax purposes because it decreases the amount of taxable income in the early years.

- Taxable income may differ from pretax income reported on the income statement. If so, the difference between the tax expense and the amount of tax actually paid is a balance sheet item, Deferred Income Taxes.

- Depletion is the process of writing off wasting assets, and amortization is the process of writing off intangible assets. The accounting for both processes is similar to depreciation, except that the credit is made directly to the asset account.

You have completed Part 7 of this program. If you think you understand the material in this part, you should now take Post Test 7, which is in the separate booklet. If you are uncertain about your understanding, you should review Part 7.

4-40. In January, Loren Company sold another motorcycle for $3,800 and delivered it to Jean Matthews. Matthews agreed to pay for the motorcycle in 30 days.

In this case revenue is recognized in the . . . [month before / same month as / month after] the related cash receipt.

month before

4-41. When revenue is recognized before the related cash receipt, as in the preceding transaction, the revenue is accompanied by the right to collect the cash, which is an Account Receivable. Thus, the entry for the sale of the motorcycle on credit was:

Dr. _____ _____ 3,800

    Cr. Sales _____ 3,800

Dr. Accounts Receivable 3,800

    Cr. Revenue 3,800

4-42. When a customer pays an entity for a credit purchase, the entity records an increase in Cash and a corresponding decrease in Accounts Receivable. Thus, when Loren Company receives a check for $3,800 from Matthews in February, Loren Company makes the following entry:

Dr. _____ 3,800

    Cr. _____ _____ . . . 3,800

Dr. Cash 3,800

    Cr. Accounts Receivable 3,800

Revenue . . . [was / was not] recognized in February.

was not

4-43. So far we have treated the cases in which

1. revenue is recognized *in the same period* as the associated cash receipt, and
2. revenue is recognized *before* the associated receipt of cash.

There remains the case in which

3. revenue is recognized _____ the associated receipt of cash.

after

INTANGIBLE ASSETS

7-67. In accordance with the asset-measurement concept, intangible items such as goodwill, trademarks, and patents are not treated as assets unless . . . [their fair value can be determined / they have been acquired at a measurable cost].

they have been acquired at a measurable cost

7-68. When intangibles are recognized as assets, their cost is written off over their service life. For example, patents have a maximum life of approximately 17 years. In no case can the life of an intangible asset exceed 40 years. The process is called **amortization.** Amortization, therefore, means . . . .

writing off the cost of intangible assets.

7-69. Company A reports $1,000,000 of trademarks on its balance sheet, but Company B reports no such item. Which statement is more likely to be correct?

1. Company A has more valuable trademarks than Company B, *or*
2. Company A has purchased trademarks, but Company B has not.

2

> **NOTE:** The Accounting treatment of trademark is similar to that of goodwill.

7-70. Three terms that refer to the writing off of an asset's cost are:

A. Depr __ __ __ __ tion, which refers to _____ (what type of?) assets,

Depreciation   plant

B. Dep __ __ tion, which refers to _____ (what type of?) assets,

Depletion   wasting

C. Amor __ __ __ __ tion, which refers to _____ (what type of?) assets.

Amortization   intangible

> **NOTE:** Although we have used the word **amortization** just for intangible assets, it is sometimes used as a general term for expensing the cost of all assets; that is, some people call **depreciation** and **depletion** special cases of amortization.

4-44. When a customer pays an entity in advance of delivery of the product, the entity has an obligation to deliver the product. This obligation is a(n) . . . [asset / liability / equity]. It is listed on the . . . [left / right] side of the balance sheet with the title **Advances from Customers.**

liability   right

4-45. Thus, when an entity receives cash in advance of delivery, it records a debit to Cash and a corresponding credit to the liability, Advances from Customers.

In March, Maypo Company received $3,000 cash in advance from a firm to prepare an advertising brochure. Write the entry that Maypo Company should make in March to record this transaction.

Dr. _____   3,000

    Cr. _____ _____ _____   3,000

Dr. Cash   3,000

    Cr. Advances from Customers   3,000

4-46. In March, Maypo Company received $3,000 in advance from a firm to prepare an advertising brochure. It delivered the brochure in June. It therefore no longer had the liability, Advances from Customers. Write the entry that should be made in June.

Dr. _____ _____ _____   3,000

    Cr. S _____ R _____   3,000

Dr. Advances from Customers . . 3,000

    Cr. Sales Revenue   3,000

March	April	May	June
Cash received	Product made		Product delivered

Revenue recognized

7-61. The book value of a plant asset represents . . . [what the asset can be sold for / that portion of the cost not yet expensed]. Therefore, the statement "book value reports what the asset is worth" is . . . [correct / incorrect].

that portion of the cost not yet expensed

incorrect
   (*This is a very common error.*)

DEPLETION

7-62. Natural resources such as coal, oil, and other minerals are called **wasting assets.** Of the following, circle those that are wasting assets.

building	natural gas	freight car
iron ore mine	cash	oil well

natural gas
iron ore mine   oil well

7-63. When the supply of oil in a well or coal in a mine is reduced, the asset is said to be **depleted.** This word, when used as the noun "dep __ __ __ ion," is the name for the process of writing off the cost of these w __ __ __ __ __ __ assets.

depletion

wasting

7-64. The . . . [depletion / depreciation] of a wasting asset is similar to the . . . [depletion / depreciation] of a plant asset. However, in accounting for **depletion,** the asset account is reduced directly. Therefore, an accumulated depletion account . . . [is / is not] ordinarily used.

depletion
depreciation

is not

7-65. Depletion is usually calculated by multiplying the quantity of the resource used in a period by a unit cost. If in 2001 Cecil Company purchased a coal mine for $3,000,000 and estimated that the mine contained 1,000,000 tons of coal, it would use a unit cost of $_____ per ton.

$3 (= $3,000,000 ÷ 1,000,000 tons)

7-66. In 2002, Cecil Company mined 100,000 tons of coal. The cost of this coal was estimated to be $3 per ton. The depletion expense in 2002 was $_____. How will the coal mine asset appear on the balance sheet for December 31, 2002?

$300,000 (= $3 * 100,000)

Coal mine . . . . $ [   ]

$2,700,000 (= $3,000,000 – $300,000)

4-47. A magazine publisher received a check for $50 in 2001 for a magazine subscription. The magazines will be delivered in 2002. Write the entry that the publisher should make in 2001.

Dr. _____ 50

    Cr. _____ _____ _____ 50

Dr. Cash	50	
Cr. Advances from Customers		50

> **NOTE:** The terms "Deferred Revenue," "Precollected Revenue," and "Unearned Revenue" are sometimes used instead of "Advances from Customers."

4-48. A publisher received $50 for a magazine subscription in 2001. In 2002, when the magazines are delivered, the publisher recognizes the $50 revenue and records a corresponding decrease in the liability, Advances from Customers.

Write the names of the accounts and the amounts for the entry that should be made in 2002.

Dr. _____ _____ _____ ☐

    Cr. _____ _____ ...... ☐

Dr. Advances from Customers ..	50	
Cr. Sales Revenue		50

4-49. The customer's advance may provide for revenue that will be earned over several future accounting periods. Suppose in 2001 a publisher received $80 for a magazine subscription, with the magazines to be delivered in 2002 and 2003. The entry for 2001 should be:

Dr. _____ .... ☐

    Cr. _____ _____ _____ ☐

Dr. Cash	80	
Cr. Advances from Customers		80

The amount of the liability at the end of 2001 would be . . . [$80 / $40 / $20 / $0].

$80

7-56. The difference between book value and the amount actually realized from a sale of a plant asset is called a **gain** (or **loss**) **on disposition of plant.** For example, if an asset whose book value is $10,000 is sold for $12,000, $_____ would be the . . . [gain / loss] on disposition of plant and would be so reported on the income statement.

$2,000 (= $12,000 − $10,000)

gain

7-57. When the asset is sold, its cost and its accumulated depreciation are removed from the accounts. For an asset that cost $40,000, had accumulated depreciation of $30,000, and sold for $12,000, the journal entry would be:

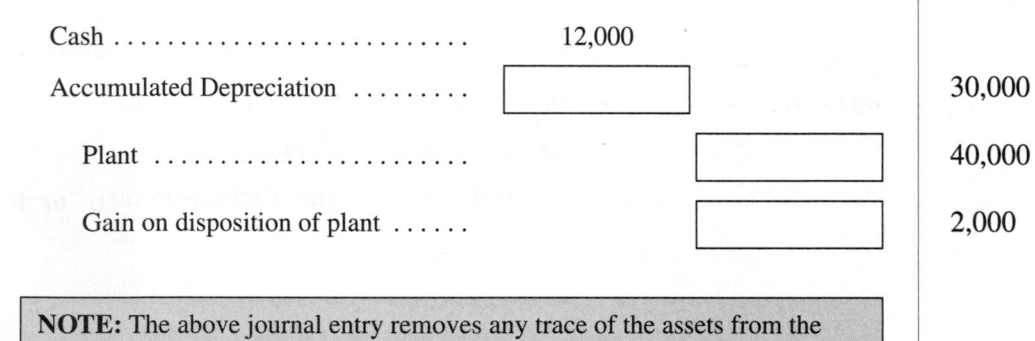

Cash	12,000	
Accumulated Depreciation		30,000
Plant		40,000
Gain on disposition of plant		2,000

> **NOTE:** The above journal entry removes any trace of the assets from the balance sheet and records the amount greater than the book value as a gain.

SIGNIFICANCE OF DEPRECIATION

7-58. The purpose of depreciation is to . . . [show the decline in an asset's value / write off a fair share of the cost of the asset in each year in which it provides service].

write off a fair share of the cost of the asset in each year in which it provides service

7-59. Actually, an asset may be as valuable at the end of a year as at the beginning. Depreciation expense for a given year . . . [represents / does not represent] a decrease in the asset's real value or usefulness during the year.

does not represent

7-60. Remember that in accounting for a plant asset, original cost is . . . [known / an estimate], service life is . . . [known / an estimate], and residual value is . . . [known / an estimate].

known   an estimate

an estimate

4-50. In 2001, a publisher received $80 for a magazine subscription, with the magazines to be delivered in 2002 and 2003. The entry for 2002 would be:

Dr. _____ _____ _____ ☐

    Cr. _____ _____ . . . . . . ☐

Dr. Advances from Customers . .   40

    Cr. Sales Revenue   40

At the end of 2002, . . . [$80 / $40 / $20 / $0] would be reported as a liability on the balance sheet.

$40

4-51. In 2001, a publisher received $80 for a magazine subscription, with the magazines to be delivered in 2002 and 2003. The entry for 2003 would be:

Dr. _____ _____ _____   40

    Cr. _____ _____   40

Dr. Advances from Customers . .   40

    Cr. Sales Revenue   40

At the end of 2003, . . . [$80 / $40 / $20 / $0] would be reported as a liability on the balance sheet.

$0

> **NOTE:** The effect of recording these transactions is to assign the total subscription of $80 to the years in which the magazine will be delivered—$40 to each year.

SERVICE REVENUE

4-52. Revenue is recognized in the period in which services are delivered. If a landlord receives cash from a tenant in January and in return permits the tenant to use an apartment in February, March, and April, the landlord recognizes revenue in . . . [January / February / March / April].

February, March, April

7-52. Refer to the following diagram:

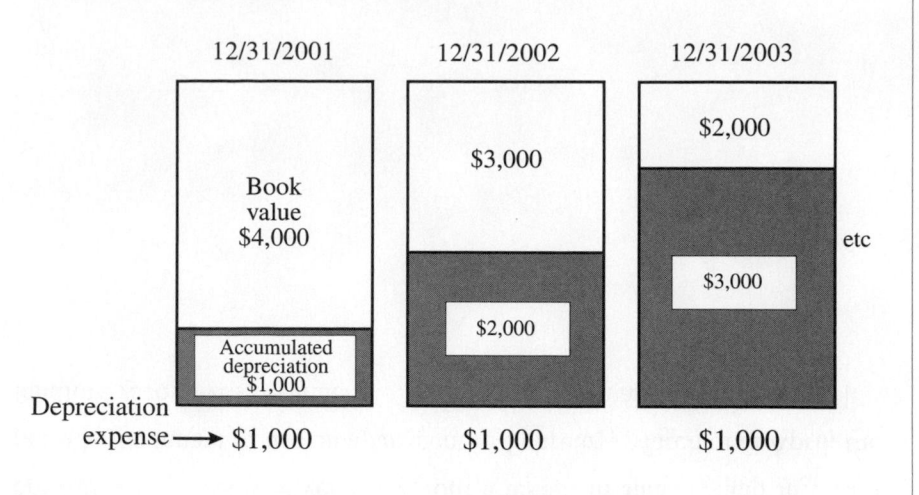

Show how the asset would be reported on the company's balance sheet at the end of 2003.

_____	$ _____
Less _____ _____ .	_____
_____ _____	_____

Plant $5,000

Less accumulated depreciation 3,000

Book value 2,000

7-53. After the cost of an asset has been completely written off as depreciation expense, no more depreciation is recorded, even though the asset continues to be used. In the example given above, the book value at the end of 2005 is zero. If the asset continued to be used in 2006, depreciation expense in 2006 would be _____.

zero

7-54. To calculate the book value of an asset, you must subtract the _____ _____ from the original _____. Book value . . . [does / does not] report the fair value of the asset.

accumulated depreciation   cost

does not

SALE OF A PLANT ASSET

7-55. The calculation of book value depends on estimates of service life and residual value. Because the actual residual value probably differs from these estimates, the amount realized from the sale of a plant asset will probably be . . . [equal to / different from] its book value.

different from

4-53. In January, a tenant paid the landlord $2,400 cash covering rent for February, March, and April. This type of revenue is called **rental revenue.** How much revenue would the landlord recognize each month, and how much liability would be reported at the end of each month?

	Rental Revenue for the month	Liability at the end of month
January	$	$
February	$	$
March	$	$
April	$	$

	Rental Revenue for the month	Liability at the end of month
January	$ 0	$2,400
February	$800	$1,600
March	$800	$ 800
April	$800	$ 0

4-54. When a bank lends money, it delivers a service; that is, the bank provides the borrower with the use of the money for a specified period of time. The bank earns revenue for the service it delivers during this period. This type of revenue is called **interest revenue.** In accordance with the realization concept, interest revenue is recognized in the period(s) . . . [in which the interest is received / in which the borrower has the use of the money].

in which the borrower has the use of the money

NOTE: The term "interest income" is sometimes used, but the amount actually is revenue, not income. Income is always a *difference* between revenue and expense.

4-55. Interest revenue is similar to rental revenue. Banks **deliver** a service when they "rent" money; landlords **deliver** a service when they rent apartments. In both cases, revenue is realized in the period(s) in which the service is d __ __ __ __ __ __ __ __ .

delivered

4-56. To summarize, accountants recognize revenue in the month *before* the related cash receipt by crediting Revenues and debiting a(n) . . . [asset / liability / equity] account entitled A __ __ __ __ __ __ __ __ R __ __ __ __ __ __ __ __ __ .

asset   Accounts
Receivable

7-49. The balance sheet for December 31, 2005, would include the following items.

Plant . . . . $ [   ]

Less _____ _____ . . . . [   ]

Book value . . . . $ [   ]

Plant	$10,000
Less accumulated depreciation	5,000
Book value	$ 5,000

The income statement for 2005 would include an item:

Depreciation expense . . . . $ [   ]

$1,000

7-50. Each year, the write-off of $1,000 of the cost of the asset is recorded with the following journal entry:

Dr. _____ _____ . . . . _____

Cr. _____ _____ . . . . _____

Depreciation Expense	1,000
Accumulated Depreciation . .	1,000

7-51. The table below shows the original cost, annual depreciation expense, accumulated depreciation (at year end), and book value (at year end) for a plant asset with an original cost of $5,000, a service life of five years, and zero residual value. Complete the amounts for 2005.

Year	Original Cost	Depreciation Expense	Accumulated Depreciation	Book Value
2001	$5,000	$1,000	$1,000	$4,000
2002	5,000	1,000	2,000	3,000
2003	5,000	1,000	3,000	2,000
2004	5,000	1,000	4,000	1,000
2005	5,000	[ ]	[ ]	[ ]

1,000   5,000   zero

What is the total amount charged as depreciation expense during the service life of the asset? $_____.

$5,000

4-57. Accountants recognize revenue in the month *after* the related cash receipt by debiting Cash and crediting a(n) . . . [asset / liability / equity] account when the cash is received. Revenue is recognized when the product is d __ __ __ __ __ __ __ __ in accordance with the r __ __ __ __ __ __ __ __ __ __ __ concept.

liability

delivered

realization

> **NOTE:** There are exceptions to the principle that revenue is recognized when a product is delivered. They involve certain types of installment sales, certain long-term contracts, and a few other special situations. They are outside the scope of this introductory treatment.

AMOUNT OF REVENUE

> **NOTE:** The realization concept describes when revenue is recognized. The conservatism concept governs both *when* and *how much* revenue is recognized. In the following frames, you will apply the conservation concept.

4-58. Loren Company sold a motorcycle to James Austin for $3,000 on credit, but Austin never paid the $3,000. Since Loren Company's assets decreased by one motorcycle but there was no actual increase in another asset, Loren Company's equity actually . . . [increased / stayed the same / decreased] as a result of this transaction. Loren Company . . . [did / did not] realize revenue from this transaction.

decreased

did not

4-59. Obviously, if Loren Company knew in advance that Austin would not pay for the motorcycle, Loren would not have delivered it. Although Loren . . . [would / would not] knowingly sell a motorcycle to someone who is not going to pay, if some customers do not pay, there is a **bad debt.** Loren . . . [must / need not] take this possibility into account in measuring its income. It does this by estimating the amount of revenue that it is **reasonably certain** to receive from all its sales during the accounting period.

would not

must

4-60. Recognizing only the amount of revenue that is reasonably certain to be received is required by the . . . [conservatism / materiality / realization] concept.

conservatism

7-46. On the balance sheet, the balance in the Accumulated Depreciation account is shown as a deduction from the original cost of the asset, and the remaining amount is called **Book Value.** For example, the listing:

```
        Plant  . . . . . . . . . . . . . . . . . . . . . . . . . . . . . . . . . $10,000
             Less accumulated depreciation  . . . . . . . . . . . .    4,000
                  Book value  . . . . . . . . . . . . . . . . . . . . . . . . $ 6,000
```

shows that the plant originally cost $_____, that $_____ of its original cost has so far been recognized as depreciation expense, and that $_____ of book value remains to be depreciated in future years. (Part of the book value may be the estimated residual value.)

$10,000 $4,000

$6,000

7-47. If the depreciation expense on this machine was $1,000 per year, we know from the above that depreciation expense has been taken for _____ (how many?) years and that it will be taken for _____ (how many?) more years in the future, assuming zero residual value.

four

six

7-48. Suppose that the ledger showed the following account balances on January 1, 2002, and that annual depreciation expense was $1,000. Enter the amounts for depreciation in 2002.

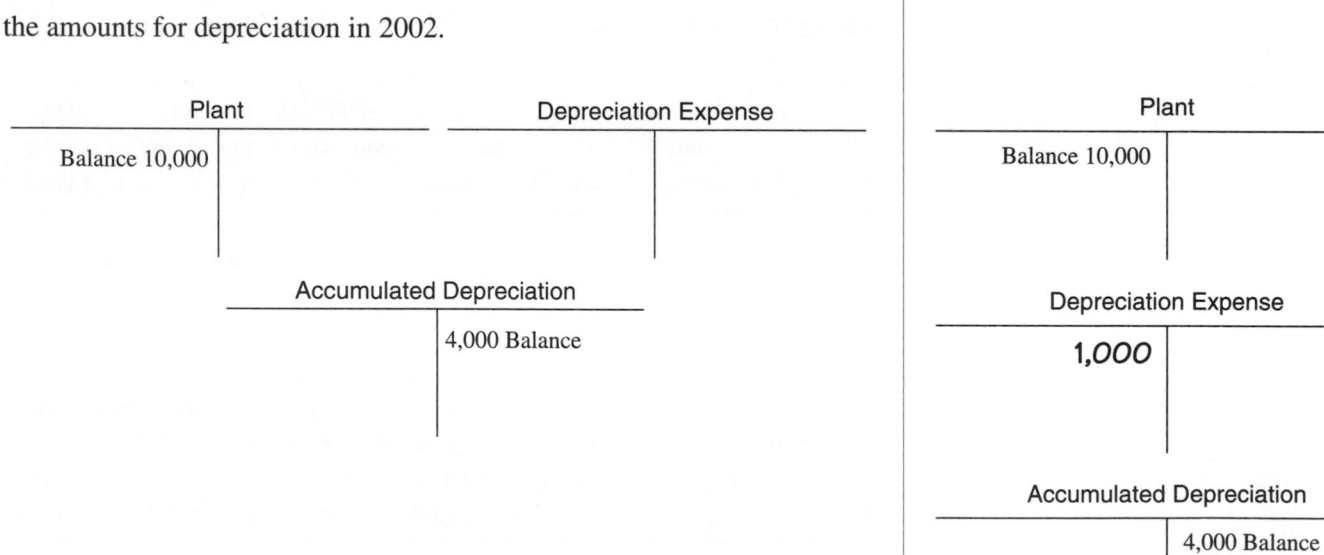

4-61. In 2001, Loren Company sold $500,000 of motorcycles to customers, all on credit. It estimated that 2% of these credit sales would never be collected; that is, they would become **bad debts.** Its estimate of bad debts for 2001 was $_____, and its increase in equity in 2001 was therefore only $_____.

$10,000 (= .02 * $500,000)
$490,000 (= $500,000 − $10,000)

4-62. Loren Company recorded each sale as revenue at the time the motorcycles were delivered. In order to measure its increase in equity properly, it must . . . [increase / decrease] the total amount of the change in equity by $_____.

decrease
$10,000

4-63. After this decrease, the amount recognized as revenue is $_____. This is the amount that is . . . [possible / reasonably certain] to be realized. This is in accordance with the . . . [conservatism / materiality] concept.

$490,000   reasonably certain
conservatism

4-64. Since the Accounts Receivable account includes amounts from customers who probably will never pay their bills, it overstates the real asset value. Thus, if the Loren Company decreases its equity by $10,000, it must also . . . [increase / decrease] its Accounts Receivable account by $10,000. Otherwise, the equality of Assets = Liabilities + Equity will not be maintained.

decrease

4-65. However, accountants usually can't decrease the Accounts Receivable account directly because they don't know *which* customers will not pay their bills. Therefore, accountants usually set up a separate account, called **Allowance for Doubtful Accounts.** They record the estimated amount of bad debts as an increase in this account. Accounts Receivable, like all asset accounts, has a . . . [debit / credit] balance. Allowance for Doubtful Accounts, which is subtracted from Accounts Receivable, therefore must have the opposite balance; that is, a . . . [debit / credit] balance.

debit

credit

7-41. Similarly, if a company purchased a three-year insurance policy in advance for $9,000 on December 31, 2001, the following journal entry would be made to record Insurance Expense in 2002.

Dr. _____ _____ . . . . _____

    Cr. _____ _____ . . . . _____

Insurance Expense 3,000

    Prepaid Expense   3,000
    (*or* Prepaid Insurance)

7-42. In accounting for depreciation, the procedure is similar. First, we recognize the appropriate amount of expense for the period. In this case the title of the expense account is D_____ Expense.

Depreciation

7-43. Next, we must recognize an equal . . . [decrease / increase] in the amount of the asset. However, accountants prefer to show the original cost of plant assets on the balance sheet at all times. Therefore, decreases in the amount of a plant asset . . . [are / are not] shown as a direct reduction in the asset amount.

decrease

are not

7-44. Instead, decreases in the asset amount of a plant asset because of depreciation expense are accumulated in a separate account called **Accumulated Depreciation.**

A decrease in an asset is always a . . . [debit / credit]. Accumulated Depreciation is a decrease in an asset, and therefore has a . . . [Dr. / Cr.] balance. (Accumulated Depreciation is called a *contra-asset* account.)

credit
Cr.

7-45. Suppose $1,000 of depreciation expense is recognized for a given year. What is the journal entry?

Dr. D _____ E _____ . . . . . . _____

    Cr. A _____ D _____ _____

Depreciation Expense 1,000

    Accumulated Depreciation . .   1,000

4-66. Although this decrease in equity theoretically resulted from the overstatement of revenue, accountants usually record it as an account called **Bad Debt Expense.** The amount recorded as Bad Debt Expense would be $_____. An increase in expense has the same effect on equity as a(n) . . . [decrease / increase] in revenue.

$10,000

decrease

4-67. The entry to record Loren Company's estimate that Bad Debt Expense should be increased by $10,000 and an Allowance for Doubtful Accounts of $10,000 should be established is:

Dr. _____ _____ _____ 10,000

    Cr. _____ _____

          _____ _____ 10,000

Dr. Bad Debt Expense 10,000

    Cr. Allowance for

        Doubtful Accounts   10,000

4-68. On December 31, 2001, Loren Company had $125,000 of Accounts Receivable before subtracting the Allowance for Doubtful Accounts. Fill in the amounts that would be reported on Loren Company's December 31, 2001, balance sheet.

Accounts receivable, gross	$	$125,000
Less Allowance for doubtful accounts . . . . –		10,000
Accounts receivable, net	$	$115,000

7-38. There are many ways of calculating accelerated depreciation amounts. The following table shows one of them. The asset has a depreciable cost of $15,000 and a service life of five years. Enter the amounts for straight-line depreciation and show whether accelerated depreciation is larger or smaller in each of the five years.

Year	Accelerated Depreciation	Straight-line Depreciation	Accelerated is		
1	$ 5,000	$_____	larger/smaller	$3,000	larger
2	4,000	_____	larger/smaller	3,000	larger
3	3,000	3,000	same	3,000	same
4	2,000	_____	larger/smaller	3,000	smaller
5	1,000	_____	larger/smaller	3,000	smaller
Total	$15,000	$ 15,000			

Accelerated depreciation is used principally in calculating taxable income. Taxable income and accounting income are not always the same, and hence the income tax paid and the income tax expense may be different. The difference becomes a liability account on the balance sheet called Deferred Income Taxes. This concept is beyond the scope of the introductory material in this text.

ACCOUNTING FOR DEPRECIATION

7-39. In Part 5 we described how certain types of assets were converted into expenses with the passage of time. When this occurs, there is a . . . [Dr. / Cr.] entry to the asset account, which shows the . . . [decrease / increase] in the amount of the asset, and there is an equal . . . [Dr. / Cr.] to the expense account.

Cr.   decrease

Dr.

7-40. For example, if an entity had a fuel oil asset of $2,000 at the beginning of March and used $500 of fuel oil during March, the entity will recognize $_____ of fuel oil expense for March, and it will also recognize an equal decrease of $_____ in the fuel oil asset. On the balance sheet of March 31, the fuel oil asset will be reported at $_____ .

$500

$500

$1,500 (= $2,000 − $500)

4-69. Sometime in 2002, Loren Company recognizes that it is never going to collect the $3,000 owed by Austin. It therefore *writes off* the bad debt. It does this by decreasing Accounts Receivable and also decreasing Allowance for Doubtful Accounts. Write the entry for this transaction.

Dr. _____ _____

_____ _____ 3,000

    Cr. _____ _____ 3,000

Dr. Allowance for

    Doubtful Accounts 3,000

    Cr. Accounts Receivable 3,000

4-70. Loren Company's equity in 2001 was reduced by the estimated bad debts on sales made in 2001, but its equity in 2002 . . . [was / was not] affected by this write-off of a bad debt.

was not
(*Since equity was decreased in 2001, it should not be decreased again for the same motorcycle.*)

4-71. In the above entry, the gross Accounts Receivable was reduced by $3,000 and the Allowance for Doubtful Accounts was also reduced by $3,000. Therefore, the write-off . . . [increased / decreased / had no effect on] the "Accounts Receivable, Net" item on the balance sheet.

had no effect on

MONETARY ASSETS

4-72. Monetary assets are cash and promises by an outside party to pay the entity a specified amount of money. Which of the following assets are monetary assets?

A. Inventory	D. Buildings
B. Accounts receivable	E. Equipment
C. Notes receivable	F. Bonds owned by the entity

B, C, and F

4-73. As with accounts receivable, other monetary assets are usually reported on the balance sheet at the amounts that are r _____

c _____ to be received. By contrast, nonmonetary assets, such as buildings and equipment, are reported at their c _____ . This is in accordance with the asset-measurement concept.

reasonably

certain

cost

7-34. Complete the following table.

If the estimated life of an asset is:	The straight-line depreciation rate is:	
2 years	[ ] %	50%
3 years	[ ] %	33-1/3%
4 years	[ ] %	25%
5 years	20%	

7-35. In the straight-line method, the amount of **depreciation expense** for a given year is found by multiplying the depreciable cost by the depreciation rate. Thus, if the depreciable cost is $9,000 and the depreciation rate is 20%, the amount of depreciation expense each year will be $_____.

$1,800 (= $9,000 * 0.20)

ACCELERATED DEPRECIATION

7-36. If you want an automobile to go faster, you press down on the accelerator. **Accelerated Depreciation** writes off the cost of an asset . . . [faster / slower] than straight-line depreciation.

faster

7-37. In accelerated depreciation, more depreciation expense is reported in the early years of the asset's service life and therefore . . . [more / less] in the later years. The total amount of depreciation expense is the same as in the straight-line method.

less

DAYS' SALES UNCOLLECTED

4-74. In Part 1 we described the current ratio, which is:

$$\frac{\text{Current a\_\_ \_\_ \_\_ \_\_ s}}{\text{Current l\_\_ \_\_ \_\_ \_\_ \_\_ \_\_ \_\_ \_\_ s}}$$

$$\frac{\text{Current assets}}{\text{Current liabilities}}$$

4-75. Another useful ratio is Days' Sales Uncollected. This is the number of days of sales that are reported in Accounts Receivable at the end of the accounting period. Sales per day are total credit sales for the year divided by 365. The formula is:

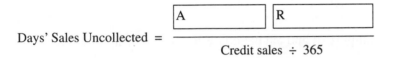

$$\text{Days' Sales Uncollected} = \frac{\boxed{A \qquad} \quad \boxed{R \qquad}}{\text{Credit sales} \div 365}$$

$$\frac{\text{Accounts Receivable}}{\text{Credit sales} \div 365}$$

4-76. Calculate the Days' Sales Uncollected ratio for Worley Company from the following data:

Accounts receivable, December 31, 2001 . . . . $50,000

Credit sales for the year 2001 . . . . $365,000

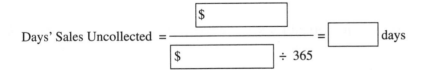

$$\text{Days' Sales Uncollected} = \frac{\boxed{\$\qquad}}{\boxed{\$\qquad} \div 365} = \boxed{\qquad} \text{ days}$$

$$\frac{\$50,000}{\$365,000 \div 365} = 50 \text{ days}$$

4-77. The Days' Sales Uncollected ratio indicates whether customers are paying their bills when they are due. If Worley Company expects customers to pay within 30 days from the date of the sale, the ratio of 50 days indicates that customers . . . [are / are not] paying on time.

are not

> **NOTE:** This is only a rough indication; it assumes that sales are made evenly throughout the year, which is not the case with seasonal sales.

STRAIGHT-LINE DEPRECIATION

7-31. The depreciation of a plant asset with a cost of $10,000, no residual value, and a five-year life, may be graphed as follows:

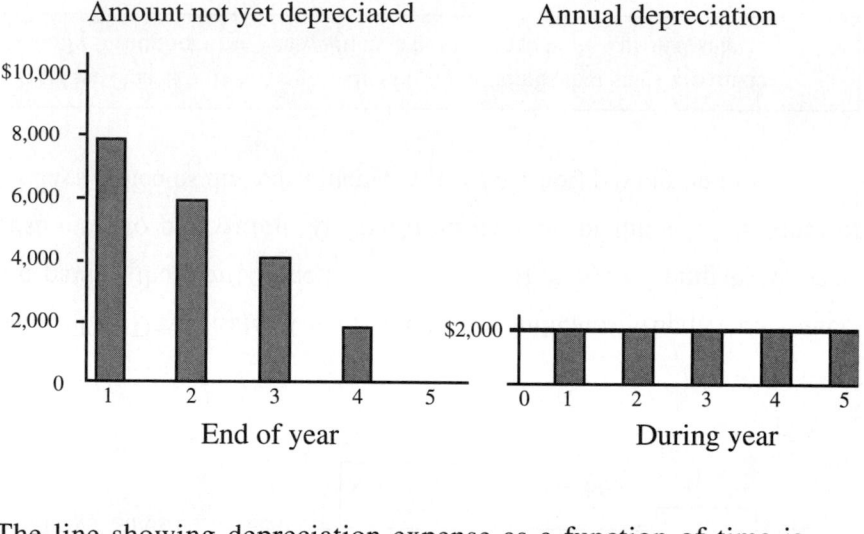

The line showing depreciation expense as a function of time is . . . [straight / vertical].

straight

7-32. Because of this, charging off an equal fraction of the asset cost each year is called the s __ __ __ __ __ __ __ __ - line method of depreciation. Most companies use this method.

straight

7-33. The percentage of cost charged off each year is called the depreciation rate. In the straight-line method, we obtain the rate by finding:

$$\frac{1}{\text{number of years of service life}}$$

For example, if an asset is to be depreciated over five years, the d _____ r _____ is _____ %.

depreciation rate   20% (1/5)

KEY POINTS TO REMEMBER

- The official accounting period is called the fiscal year, but financial statements can be prepared for shorter periods. They are called interim statements.

- Accrual accounting measures revenues and expenses during an accounting period and the difference between them, which is net income. Accrual accounting is more complicated, but more useful, than accounting only for cash receipts and cash payments.

- The conservatism concept: Recognize increases in equity when they are reasonably certain, but recognize decreases as soon as they are reasonably possible.

- The materiality concept: Disregard trivial matters, but disclose all important matters.

- The realization concept: Revenue is usually recognized when goods and services are delivered.

- If revenue is recognized before the cash receipt, an asset, Accounts Receivable, is debited (increased). If cash is received before revenue is recognized, a liability, Advances from Customers, is credited (increased). The liability is debited (decreased) in the period(s) in which revenue is recognized.

- The equity and accounts receivable balances in a period are reduced by estimated bad debt losses. A Bad Debt Expense account is used to record the decrease in equity. When specific bad debts are later discovered, Accounts Receivable is reduced, but revenue is unaffected.

- The days' sales uncollected ratio is

$$\frac{\text{Accounts receivable}}{\text{Credit sales} \div 365}$$

It indicates whether customers are paying their bills on time.

You have completed Part 4 of this program. If you think you understand the material in this part, you should now take Post Test 4, which is in the separate booklet. If you are uncertain about your understanding, you should review Part 4.

The post test will serve both to test your comprehension and to review the highlights of Part 4. After taking the post test, you may find that you are unsure about certain points. You should review these points before going on to Part 5.

7-28. The difference between the cost of a plant asset and its residual value is called the **depreciable cost.** Thus, if an automobile purchased for $30,000 is expected to have a five-year life and to have a residual value of $5,000 at the end of that life, $30,000 is the original _____ and $25,000 is the _____ _____.

cost (or gross cost)

depreciable cost

7-29. Here is a list of factors that are relevant to the depreciation of an asset:

1. original cost
2. residual value
3. service life

Which factors are used in arriving at the depreciable cost?. . . . .   1 and 2

The amount of depreciation expense in a given year? . . . .   1, 2, and 3

Which factors are estimates? . . . .   2 and 3

> **NOTE:** There are many methods of calculating the amount that is to be recorded as depreciation expense in each year of the estimated service life. In the following sections we describe three of them:
>
> 1. Units-of-production depreciation
> 2. Straight-line depreciation
> 3. Accelerated depreciation

UNITS-OF-PRODUCTION DEPRECIATION

7-30. In the units-of-production method, a cost per unit of production is calculated, and depreciation expense for a year is found by multiplying this unit cost by the number of units that the asset produced in that year.

Grady Company purchased a truck in 2001 for $44,000. It estimated that the truck would provide services for 100,000 miles and would have a residual value of $4,000.

Its depreciable cost was $_____.

$40,000 (= $44,000 − $4,000)

Its estimated cost per mile was $_____.

$0.40 (= $40,000 ÷ 100,000)

In 2002, the truck was driven 15,000 miles. Its depreciation expense in 2002 was $_____.

$6,000 (= $0.40 * $15,000)

Part 5

Expense Measurement; The Income Statement

Learning Objectives

In this part you will learn:

- The difference between "expense" and "expenditure."
- How the expenses of a period are measured.
- The last of the nine basic accounting concepts:
    - The matching concept.
- The meaning of items reported on an income statement.
- Methods of analyzing an income statement.

5-1. In Part 4 you learned that the revenues recognized in an accounting period were not necessarily associated with the cash receipts in that period. If $1,000 of goods were delivered to a customer in August, and the customer paid cash for these goods in September, revenue would be recognized in . . . [August / September].

August

5-2. Revenues are . . . [increases / decreases] in equity during an accounting period. Expenses are . . . [increases / decreases] in equity during an accounting period. Just as revenues in a period are not necessarily the same as cash receipts in that period, the expenses of a period . . . [are / are not] necessarily the same as the cash payments in that period.

increases
decreases

are not

7-23. To summarize:

1. Depreciation is the process of converting the cost of an asset into expense over its service life.

2. This process recognizes that an asset gradually loses its usefulness.

3. An asset can lose its usefulness for either of two reasons:

    a. . . . .   it wears out

    b. . . . .   it becomes obsolete

4. The asset's service life is the . . . [longer / shorter] of these two   shorter
    causes.

7-24. In the summary above, no mention was made of market value. Depreciation . . . [is / is not] related to changes in the market value of an   is not
asset. This is consistent with the _____ - _____   asset-measurement
concept.

7-25. In some cases, an entity expects to be able to sell the plant asset at the end of its service life. The amount that it expects to sell it for is called its **residual value.** If an entity buys a truck for $60,000 and expects to sell it for $10,000 five years later, the estimated residual value is

$_____. $10,000

7-26. In most cases, an entity expects that a plant asset will be worthless at the end of its service life. If so, its residual value is _____   zero
(how much?).

> **NOTE:** Residual value, as such, does not appear in the accounts. It is merely an estimated number used to calculate depreciation.

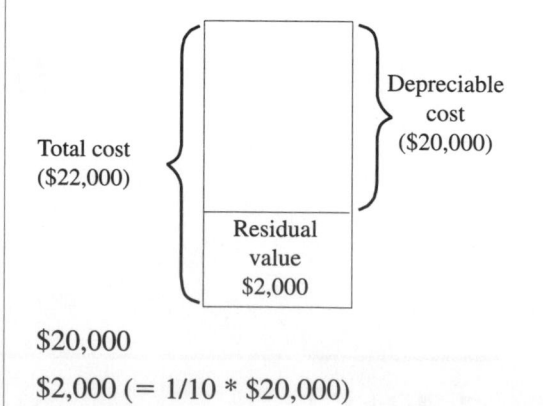

7-27. Suppose a restaurant oven that cost $22,000 is expected to have a residual value of $2,000 at the end of its 10-year life. In this case, the total amount of depreciation that should be recorded during the service life of the asset is only $_____. The depreciation expense for $20,000
each of the 10 years would be $_____. $2,000 (= 1/10 * $20,000)

EXPENSE AND EXPENDITURE

5-3. When an entity acquires goods or services, it makes an **expenditure.** In August, Mogul Shop purchased goods for its inventory at a cost of $1,000, paying cash; it had an e _____ of $1,000 in August. It would record this transaction with the following journal entry:

expenditure

Dr. I _____ 1,000

    Cr. C _____ 1,000

Inventory 1,000

    Cash   1,000

5-4. If in August, Mogul Shop purchased $2,000 of goods for inventory, agreeing to pay in 30 days, it had an e _____ of $2,000 in August. Accounts Payable, which is a liability account, increased. Mogul would record this transaction with the following journal entry:

expenditure

Dr. I _____ 2,000

    Cr. A _____ P _____ .. 2,000

Inventory 2,000

    Accounts Payable   2,000

5-5. Thus, an expenditure results either in a decrease in the asset C _____ or an increase in a l _____, such as Accounts Payable.

Cash   liability

> **NOTE:** Occasionally an expenditure results in a decrease in an asset other than cash. For example, when an old automobile is traded in for a new automobile, part of the expenditure is the decrease in the asset, Automobiles.

5-6. Mogul Shop had e _____ s of $3,000 in August for the purchase of goods for inventory. If $500 of these goods were sold in August, there was an **expense** in August of $500. The remaining $2,500 of goods are still in inventory at the end of August; they therefore are an **asset.** Thus, the expenditures of a period are either _____ of the period or _____ s at the end of the period.

expenditures

expenses   assets

7-17. When a machine or other item of plant is acquired, we . . . [know / do not know] how long it actually will be of service. Therefore, we . . . [can know with certainty / must estimate] its service life.

do not know

must estimate

7-18. Since some portion of a plant asset is used up during each year of its service life, a portion of the cost of the asset is treated as a(n) . . . [revenue / expense] in each year. For example, suppose a machine is purchased at a cost of $50,000. It has an estimated service life of five years and will be worthless then. It would be reasonable to charge _____ (what fraction?), or $_____ as expense in each of the five years.

expense

1/5 $10,000 (= 1/5 * $50,000)

7-19. The portion of the cost of a plant asset that is recognized as an expense during each year of its estimated service life is called **depreciation.** The $10,000 recorded as an expense during each one of the five years of service life of the machine that cost $50,000 is called the _____ expense for that year.

depreciation

7-20. A plant asset can become useless for either of two reasons: (1) it may wear out physically, or (2) it may become obsolete (i.e., no longer useful). The latter reason is called **obsolescence.** Loss of usefulness because of the development of improved equipment, changes in style, or other causes not related to the physical condition of the asset are examples of _____ .

obsolescence

7-21. The **service life** of an asset considers both physical wear and obsolescence. The service life is the shorter of the two periods. Thus an asset with an estimated physical life of ten years that is estimated to become obsolete in five years has an estimated service life of . . . [five / ten] years.

five

7-22. Since depreciation considers obsolescence, it is . . . [correct / not correct] to regard depreciation and obsolescence as two different things.

not correct

5-7. Mogul Shop sold the remaining $2,500 of goods in September. In September it had an . . . [expenditure / expense] of $2,500, but it did not have any . . . [expenditure / expense] for these goods in September.

expense

expenditure

5-8. In August, Mogul Shop paid an employee $2,000 cash for services rendered in August. It had both an _____ and an _____ of $2,000 for labor services in August.

expense

expenditure
  (*either order*)

5-9. When an asset is used up or consumed in the operations of the business, an expense is incurred. Thus, an asset gives rise to an . . . [expenditure / expense] when it is acquired, and to an . . . [expenditure / expense] when it is consumed.

expenditure

expense

5-10. Suppose that Irwin Company purchased a supply of fuel oil in 2001, paying $10,000 cash. No fuel oil was consumed in 2001. In 2002, $8,000 of fuel oil was consumed, and in 2003, $2,000 was consumed. There was an expenditure in _____ (when?), and there were expenses in _____ (when?).

2001

2002 and 2003

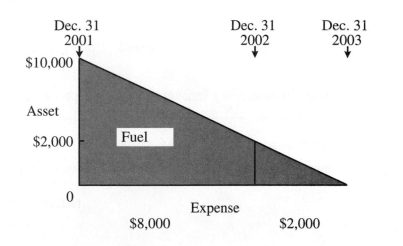

5-11. Between the time of their purchase and the time of their consumption, the resources of a business are assets. Thus, when fuel oil is purchased, there is an expenditure. The fuel oil is an _____ until consumed. When consumed, it becomes an _____ .

asset

expense

7-12. Even though the entity does not own the item, a capital lease is treated like other plant assets. A capital lease is an exception to the general rule that assets are property or property rights that are ＿＿＿＿＿ by the entity.

owned

> **NOTE:** Special rules apply to accounting for capital leases. They are beyond the scope of this introductory treatment.

DEPRECIATION

7-13. Except in rare cases, land retains its usefulness indefinitely. Land therefore continues to be reported on the balance sheet at its acquisition cost, in accordance with the ＿＿＿＿＿ - ＿＿＿＿＿ concept. This is because land is a . . . [monetary / nonmonetary] asset.

asset-measurement
nonmonetary

If Hanover Hospital purchased a plot of land in 1980 at a cost of $100,000, it would have been reported at $＿＿＿＿＿ on the December 31, 1980, balance sheet. If Hanover Hospital still owned the land in 2002, and its market value then was $300,000, it would be reported on the December 31, 2002, balance sheet at . . . [$100,000 / $300,000].

$100,000

$100,000

7-14. Unlike land, plant assets eventually become useless. They have a(n) . . . [limited / unlimited] life.

limited

7-15. Plant assets will become completely useless at some future time. At that time, the item is no longer an asset. Usually this process occurs gradually; that is, a portion of the asset is used up in each year of its life, until finally it is scrapped or sold and therefore is no longer ＿＿＿ful to the entity. At that time, it . . . [is / is not] an asset.

useful
is not

7-16. The period of time over which a plant asset is estimated to be of **service** to the company is called its s ＿＿＿＿＿＿ life.

service

5-12. Irwin Company purchased a two-year supply of fuel oil in 2001, paying $10,000. None of it was consumed in 2001, $8,000 was consumed during 2002, and $2,000 was consumed in 2003. The balance sheet item for the asset Fuel Oil Inventory will show the following amounts:

As of December 31, 2001 .... $	$10,000
As of December 31, 2002 .... $	$ 2,000
As of December 31, 2003 .... $	$ 0

5-13. Irwin Company purchased a two-year supply of fuel oil in 2001, paying $10,000. None was consumed in 2001, $8,000 was consumed in 2002, and $2,000 was consumed in 2003. The item Fuel Oil Expense on the income statements will be as follows:

For the year 2001 .... $	$ 0
For the year 2002 .... $	$8,000
For the year 2003 .... $	$2,000

5-14. Over the life of a business, most expenditures . . . [will / will not] become expenses, but in a single accounting period, expenses . . . [are / are not] necessarily the same as expenditures.

will

are not

UNEXPIRED AND EXPIRED COSTS

5-15. Expenditures result in costs. When inventory or other assets are acquired, they are recorded at their acquisition c __ __ __ . Expenses are the c __ __ __ of the resources used up in an accounting period.

cost

cost

5-16. Costs that are used up or consumed in a period are e __ __ __ __ __ __ s. Costs that are represented by resources on hand at the end of the period are a __ __ __ __ s.

expenses

assets

7-8. If an entity constructs a machine or a building with its own person-nel, all costs incurred in construction are included in the asset amount.

Thayer Company built a new building for its own use. It spent $400,000 in materials, $1,600,000 in salaries to workers directly engaged in the building's construction, $600,000 to purchase services, and $300,000 in overhead costs related to the building. This building should be recorded in the accounts at its cost, $_____.

$2,900,000 (= $400,000 + $1,600,000 + $600,000 + $300,000)

CAPITAL LEASES

7-9. Most assets are *owned* by the entity. When an entity leases (i.e., rents) a building, a machine, or other tangible item, the item is owned by someone else (the **lessor**); the entity . . . [does / does not] own it. In other words, most leased items . . . [are / are not] assets of the entity that leases them (the **lessee**).

does not

are not

7-10. However, if an entity leases an item for a long period of time, it has as much control over the use of that item as if it owned it. A lease for a long time—almost the whole life of the asset—is called a **capital lease.** Because the entity controls the item for almost its whole life, a c _ _ _ _ _ _ _ l _ _ _ _ is recorded as an asset.

capital lease

7-11. The amount recorded for a capital lease is the amount the entity would have paid if it had purchased the item rather than leased it. If an entity leased a machine for 10 years, agreeing to pay $10,000 per year, and if the purchase price of this machine was $70,000, this c _ _ _ _ _ _ _ l _ _ _ _ would be recorded as an asset at an amount of . . . [$70,000 / $100,000], as in this entry:

capital lease
$70,000

Capital Lease . . . . _____

70,000

    Lease Obligation . . . . _____

70,000

5-17. Costs that have been consumed are gone; they have **expired.** Costs of resources still on hand are **unexpired.** You will find it useful to think of expenses as . . . [expired / unexpired] costs and assets as . . . [expired / unexpired] costs.

expired   unexpired

5-18. Irwin Company purchased $10,000 of fuel oil in 2001, consumed $8,000 of it in 2002, and consumed $2,000 of it in 2003. At the end of 2001, the total expenditure of $10,000 was an . . . [asset / expense] because none of the cost had expired. In 2002, $8,000 of the cost expired, and $8,000 was therefore an . . . [asset / expense] in 2002. At the end of 2002, $2,000 was an unexpired cost and therefore an . . . [asset / expense]. The remaining $2,000 expired in 2003, so it was an . . . [asset / expense] in 2003.

asset

expense

asset

expense

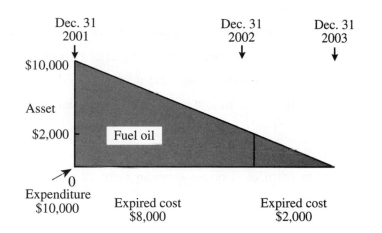

MATCHING CONCEPT

5-19. An important task of the accountant is to measure the net income of an accounting period. Net income is the difference between r __ __ __ __ __ __ s and e __ __ __ __ __ __ __ s of the period. Expenses are . . . [expired / cash] costs.

revenues   expenses

expired

5-20. As you learned in Part 4, the concept governing the recognition of revenues of a period is the r __ __ __ __ __ __ __ __ __ __ concept; revenue is recognized in the period in which goods or services are d __ __ __ __ __ __ ed.

realization

delivered

7-3. On the balance sheet, tangible noncurrent assets are often labeled **fixed assets,** or **property, plant,** and **equipment.** Equipment is a . . . [current / noncurrent] and . . . [tangible / intangible] asset.

noncurrent   tangible

7-4. For brevity, we shall use the word **plant** for all tangible noncurrent assets except land. Thus, buildings, equipment, and furniture are items of _____. These assets are expected to be useful for longer than _____ _____.

plant

one year

ACCOUNTING FOR ACQUISITIONS

7-5. When an item of plant is acquired, it is recorded in the accounts at its _____ (what value?). This is because it is a . . . [monetary / nonmonetary] asset.

cost

nonmonetary

7-6. The cost of an asset includes all costs incurred to make the asset ready for its intended use.

Bird Corporation paid $50,000 for a plot of land. It also paid $1,500 as a broker's fee, $600 for legal fees, and $5,000 to tear down the existing structures in order to make the land ready for a new building. The land should be recorded in the accounts at an amount of $_____.

$57,100 (= $50,000 + $1,500 + $600 + $5,000)
(Note: Some accountants charge the $5,000 as a cost of the new building.)

7-7. Transportation and installation costs are usually included as part of equipment cost.

Plymouth Bank purchased a computer for $40,000. The bank also paid $200 in freight charges and $2,000 in installation charges. This equipment should be recorded in the accounts at its cost, $_____.

$42,200 (= $40,000 + $200 + $2,000)

5-21. The concept governing the recognition of expenses of a period is the **matching** concept. It is that **costs associated with the revenues of a period are** . . . [cash payments / expenses] **of that period.**

expenses

5-22. To illustrate, consider an automobile that Bryan Company, an automobile dealer, purchased for $15,000 in March and sold (i.e., delivered) for $18,000 in May. At the end of March, the automobile was in the Bryan Company inventory, so its cost was . . . [expired / unexpired]. At the end of April, its cost was . . . [expired / unexpired].

unexpired
unexpired

5-23. Bryan Company purchased an automobile for $15,000 in March and sold it for $18,000 in May.

In May, Bryan Company recognizes $18,000 of _____ from the sale of this automobile. It must m __ __ __ __ the $15,000 of cost with the revenue from the sale of the same automobile. Thus, its expense in May is $15,000. The $18,000 of revenue and the $15,000 of expense relate to the same automobile. The expense **matches** the revenue.

revenue
match

OTHER ASSETS THAT WILL BECOME EXPENSES

5-24. When products are delivered, their costs are matched with revenues in the period in which the sale takes place. These costs become expenses of that period. This is one application of the m __ __ __ __ __ __ __ __ concept. Other costs associated with activities of the current period are also expenses, even though they are not directly related to the products delivered in the period.

matching

5-25. If expenditures were made in an earlier period, the unexpired costs are a __ __ __ __ __ s until the period in which the expense is recognized. We shall consider several examples. The first is an intangible asset.

assets

Part 7

Noncurrent Assets and Depreciation

Learning Objectives

In this part you will learn:

- How plant assets are recorded in the accounts.
- The meaning and significance of straight-line and accelerated depreciation.
- How depreciation is recorded.
- The meaning of depletion and how it is recorded.
- How intangible assets are recorded.

NONCURRENT ASSETS

7-1. Earlier, you learned that current assets are cash or items likely to be converted to cash within one _____ (what time period?). Evidently, **noncurrent** assets are expected to be of use to the entity for longer than _____ _____.

year

one year

7-2. Tangible assets are assets that can be touched. Intangible assets are assets that have no physical substance (other than pieces of paper) but give the entity valuable rights. Which of the following are tangible assets?

Current Assets	Noncurrent Assets
1. Account receivable	5. Land
2. Notes receivable	6. Goodwill
3. Inventory	7. Buildings
4. Prepaid rent	8. Investment in another entity

3, 5, and 7
(*Although a note receivable is shown by a paper that can be touched, the asset is the sum of money that is promised. This is an intangible asset.*)

5-26. A **tangible asset** has physical substance; an **intangible asset** does not have physical substance. Buildings, equipment, and inventories of goods are . . . [tangible / intangible] assets. The protection provided by an insurance policy is a(n) . . . [tangible / intangible] asset.

tangible
intangible

5-27. The general name for intangible assets that will become expenses in a future period is **prepaid expenses.** The asset account may identify the particular type of prepaid expense. Thus, the name of the asset account that shows the cost incurred for insurance protection in future periods is P _____ Insurance.

Prepaid

5-28. Bryan Company purchased a two-year insurance policy on December 31, 2001, for $2,000.

The effect of this expenditure is a decrease in Cash and an increase in the asset Prepaid Insurance. Record the journal entry for this transaction.

Dr. _____ _____ 2,000

    Cr. _____ 2,000

Prepaid Insurance 2,000

    Cash 2,000

5-29. Bryan Company purchased a two-year insurance policy on December 31, 2001, for $2,000.

During 2002 Bryan Company used up half of this insurance protection, thereby incurring $1,000 of insurance expense. The effect on the accounts in 2002 is a decrease in the asset Prepaid Insurance and an increase in Insurance Expense. Record the journal entry for 2002.

Dr. _____ _____ . . . . . . _____

    Cr. _____ _____ . . . . . . _____

Insurance Expense 1,000

    Prepaid Insurance 1,000

On December 31, 2002, the balance in the asset account, Prepaid Insurance, was $_____.

$1,000

- If the fair value (i.e., market value) of items in inventory decreases below their cost, the inventory is written down to fair value.

- The cost of goods produced in a manufacturing company is the sum of their direct materials cost, direct labor cost, and production overhead cost.

- Period costs are costs that are charged as expenses in the period in which the costs were incurred. Product costs become Cost of Sales in the period in which the products are sold, which may be later than the period in which the products were manufactured.

- Overhead is charged to products by means of an overhead rate, such as a rate per direct labor dollar.

- The inventory turnover ratio shows how many times the inventory turned over during a year.

You have now completed Part 6 of this program. If you think you have understood the material in this part, you should now take Post Test 6, which is in the separate booklet. If you are uncertain about your understanding, you should review Part 6.

The post test will serve both to test your comprehension and to review the highlights of Part 6. After taking the post test, you may find that you are unsure about certain points. You should review these points before going on to Part 7.

5-30. Bryan Company purchased a two-year insurance policy on December 31, 2001, for $2,000.

During 2003 Bryan Company received the remaining $1,000 of insurance protection. Make the journal entry for 2003.

Dr. _____ _____ . . . . _____

Cr. _____ _____ . . . . . . _____

Insurance Expense	. . . .	1,000	
Prepaid Insurance	. . . .		1,000

On December 31, 2003, the amount of insurance protection has completely expired. The balance in the Prepaid Insurance account on that date therefore was $_____.

$0

> **NOTE:** If you were uncertain about the responses to these frames, refer back to Frames 5-10 through 5-13.

5-31. Similarly, if Carter Company made an advance payment of $1,800 to its landlord on January 31 for two months' rent, its asset account P__ __ __ __ __ __ Rent would have a balance of $_____ on January 31, a balance of $_____ on February 28, and a balance of $_____ on March 31. Its rent expense would be $_____ in February and $_____ in March.

Prepaid $1,800
$900
$0
$900 $900

5-32. Buildings and equipment also benefit future periods. They are assets like Prepaid Insurance and Prepaid Rent, except that they usually have a longer life and therefore benefit . . . [more / fewer] future periods. The amount reported as an asset on the balance sheet is the . . . [expired / unexpired] cost as of the date of the balance sheet.

more
unexpired

5-33. Also, as with insurance and rent, the amount of building and equipment cost that is reported as an expense in each period is the amount of . . . [expired / unexpired] cost in that period.

expired

6-66. Cost of sales for 2001 was $1,000,000. Inventory on December 31, 2001, was $200,000. Calculate the inventory turnover ratio to determine how many times the inventory turned over in 2001.

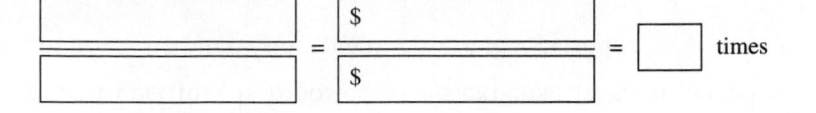

$$\frac{\text{Cost of sales}}{\text{Inventory}} = \frac{\$1,000,000}{\$200,000} = 5 \text{ times}$$

6-67. Slow-moving inventory ties up capital and increases the risk that the goods will become obsolete. Thus, an inventory turnover of five times is generally . . . [better / worse] than an inventory turnover of four times. However, if inventory is too small, orders from customers may not be filled promptly, which can result in lost sales revenue. This would reduce . . . [cash receipts / income / both cash and income].

better

both cash and income

6-68. Look back at the calculation of the inventory turnover ratio. The turnover ratio can be increased either by selling . . . [more / less] goods with the same level of inventory or by having . . . [more / less] inventory for the same amount of sales volume.

more

less

KEY POINTS TO REMEMBER

- If an entity has no record of the cost of the specific items that were sold during a period, it deduces Cost of Sales by (1) adding purchases to the beginning inventory, which gives the goods available for sale, and (2) subtracting the cost of the ending Inventory.

- In doing this, the entity must make an assumption about which items were sold.

- The First-In First-Out (FIFO) method assumes that the oldest items are the first to be sold.

- The Last-In First-Out (LIFO) method assumes that the most recently purchased items are the first to be sold. In periods of rising prices, it results in a higher Cost of Sales and hence a lower taxable income than the FIFO method.

- The average-cost method charges both Cost of Sales and the ending Inventory at the average cost of the goods available for sale.

- The inventory method that a company selects **does not necessarily reflect the physical flow of its goods.**

5-34. The expired cost for buildings and equipment is called **Depreciation Expense.** If Bryan Company bought a machine for $5,000 and expected it to provide service for five years, the amount of expired cost in each year probably would be 1/5 of $5,000. In each of the five years D _ _ _ _ _ _ _ _ _ _ _ _ E _ _ _ _ _ _ _ would be reported as $_____. Accounting for depreciation is discussed in more detail in Part 7.

Depreciation Expense
$1,000

EXPENSES THAT CREATE LIABILITIES

> **NOTE:** We have described expenditures that first were assets and then became expenses as the costs expired. We now describe expenses for which the related expenditures are liabilities.

5-35. Amounts earned by the employees of Eastman Company for services performed in 2001 are e _ _ _ _ _ _ _ s of 2001. If Eastman paid its employees one week after the week they worked, the amounts earned in the last week of 2001 would be a cash disbursement in _____ (what year?).

Expenses

2002

5-36. Employees of Eastman Company earned $10,000 in the last week of 2001, for which they were paid in 2002. The $10,000 was . . . [an expense / an expenditure / both an expense and an expenditure] in 2001.

both an expense and an expenditure

On December 31, 2001, Eastman Company owed its employees $10,000. It would report a l _ _ _ _ _ _ _ _ y of $10,000 on its December 31, 2001, balance sheet.

liability

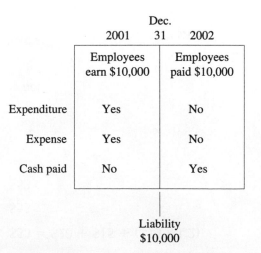

	Dec. 2001	31 2002
	Employees earn $10,000	Employees paid $10,000
Expenditure	Yes	No
Expense	Yes	No
Cash paid	No	Yes

Liability
$10,000

6-62. If a certain pair of shoes required $20 of direct material cost, $15 of direct labor cost, and overhead at a cost of $1.20 per dollar of direct labor, its total cost would be $_____. The Inventory cost of these shoes would be $_____. When they were sold, the Cost of Sales of these shoes would be $_____.

$53 = $20 + $15 + ($15 * 1.2)

$53

$53

6-63. Although $53 is reported as the "actual" cost of this pair of shoes, it cannot represent the actual overhead cost. By definition, it . . . [is / is not] possible to determine the actual indirect cost of a product. The overhead rate does charge products with what is believed to be a *fair share* of their cost. For this reason, the process of *allocating* overhead costs to products is more complex than the scope of this book.

is not

> **NOTE:** There are several other methods of assigning overhead costs to products. One of these, called activity-based costing, assigns indirect or overhead costs on the basis of relative activities. This process looks at the *cost drivers* associated with overhead activities.

INVENTORY TURNOVER

6-64. In earlier parts we described ratios and percentages that are useful in analyzing financial statements. Find the gross margin percentage from the following facts:

$$\frac{\$\ 600,000}{\$1,500,000} = \text{_____} \% \text{ Gross margin}$$

$$\frac{\text{Gross margin}}{\text{Sales (or Sales revenue)}} = 40\% \text{ Gross margin}$$

6-65. A useful ratio for analyzing inventory is the **inventory turnover ratio.** This ratio shows how many times the inventory turned over during a year. It is found by dividing Cost of Sales for a period by I _____ at the end of the period (or by the average inventory during the period).

Inventory

5-37. Liabilities for expenses incurred but not yet paid for are called **accrued liabilities.** Account titles may describe the nature of the liability, in this case A __ __ __ __ __ __ Salaries.

Accrued

5-38. In the last week of 2001, Eastman Company had a salary expense of $10,000, which was not paid to its employees. Write the journal entry for this transaction.

Dr. _____ _____ .... _____

Cr. _____ _____ ... _____

Salary Expense 10,000

    Accrued Salaries 10,000

> **NOTE:** Employees are not paid the total amount that they earn. Part of their salary is withheld by the employer, who pays it to the federal government for income taxes. Amounts are also deducted for social security taxes and for other reasons. We shall disregard these complications and assume that total earnings are paid in cash to the employees.

5-39. In January 2002, Eastman Company employees were paid the $10,000 owed them for work done in 2001. This payment decreases the liability Accrued Salaries. The journal entry for this transaction is:

Dr. _____ _____ .... _____

Cr. _____ .... _____

Accrued Salaries 10,000

    Cash 10,000

FRINGE BENEFITS

5-40. Many companies agree to pay employees a pension when they retire. Employees earn the right to their pension benefits when they work. Therefore, if an employee earns a $2,000 pension benefit in 2001 because he or she worked in 2001, the $2,000 is an expense in . . . [2001 / when he or she retires]. It is a liability in . . . [2001 / when he or she retires]. The liability is called **Accrued Pensions.**

2001

2001

6-57. This entry included only $400,000 of overhead costs, although $480,000 of overhead costs were actually incurred in the year 2002. The Cost of Sales amount . . . [was / was not] the same as the amount of cost actually incurred in the year 2002.

was not

6-58. . . . [Period / Product] costs reduce income in the period in which the costs were incurred. . . . [Period / Product] costs reduce income in the period in which the product is sold, which often is a later period.

Period

Product

OVERHEAD RATES

6-59. By definition, **direct material** and **direct labor** costs can be traced *directly* to the products for which they were incurred; the cost accounting system does this. However, production overhead, which is an **indirect** cost, cannot be so traced. The cost of heating a shoe factory . . . [can / cannot] be traced directly to the cost of manufacturing each pair of shoes made in the factory. Assigning these indirect costs to products requires the use of an **overhead rate.**

cannot

6-60. The overhead rate is a rate per direct labor dollar, per direct labor hour, per machine hour, or some other measure of volume. If Lee Shoe Company expected to incur $480,000 of production overhead costs in the year 2002, and it expected that direct labor costs in the year 2002 would be $400,000, it would establish an overhead rate of $_____ per direct labor dollar.

$1.20 (480,000/400,000)

6-61. This overhead rate would be used to find the overhead cost of each pair of shoes worked on. If an actual pair of shoes required $10 of direct labor cost, its overhead cost would be recorded as $_____.

$12

5-41. Joan Eaton earned a pension benefit of $2,000 in 2001. She had earned similar benefits in earlier years. The journal entry for this transaction is:

Dr. Pension Expense 2,000

    Cr. _____ _____ 2,000   Accrued Pensions

5-42. Joan Eaton retired on December 31, 2001. She will be paid a pension of $10,000 in 2002. The journal entry for the 2002 payment is:

Dr. _____ _____ 10,000   Accrued Pensions

    Cr. Cash 10,000

> **NOTE:** Many companies transfer amounts earned for pensions to an insurance company or bank, which makes the actual payments. The effect on the company's financial position is nevertheless the same as that illustrated in the above journal entries.

5-43. Many companies agree to pay for health care or other benefits to retired employees. These fringe benefits are called **Other Post Employment Benefits,** abbreviated to the initials ___ __ __ .   OPEB

5-44. OPEB are accounted for in the same way as pensions; that is, the expense is incurred . . . [in the years in which the employee earns the right to them / when the benefits are paid]. The liability is incurred . . . [in the years in which the employee earns the right to them / when the benefits are paid]. When the benefit is paid, there . . . [is / is not] an expense.

in the years in which the employee earns the right to them

in the years in which the employee earns the right to them
is not

6-53. The process of assigning production costs to products is called **cost accounting.** The assignment of costs to various services in banks, schools, hotels, and all types of service organizations also involves c _ _ _ a _ _ _ _ _ _ _ _ _ _ . We shall describe some of its major aspects.

cost accounting

PRODUCT COSTS AND PERIOD COSTS

6-54. Costs are divided into two categories; they are treated differently for **purposes of accounting:**

1. **product costs**—those that are associated with the production of products, and
2. **period costs**—those that are associated with the sales and general activities of the accounting period.

For example, the cost of heating the offices of the sales department would be considered a . . . [product / period] cost. The cost of heating the production plant itself would be a . . . [product / period] cost.

period
product

6-55. Overhead costs that are classified as product costs are added to direct labor costs and direct material costs to find the total cost that is added to the Inventory account. If Lee Shoe Company incurred $480,000 of production overhead costs in the year 2002, these costs would be added to inventory by this journal entry:

Dr. _____ 480,000

Inventory

    Cr. Various overhead accounts 480,000

6-56. Costs are moved from Inventory to Cost of Sales when the products are sold. If in the year 2002 Lee Shoe Company sold shoes with direct material and labor costs of $1,000,000 and overhead costs of $400,000, the entry would be:

Dr. Cost of Sales . . . . _____

. . . . 1,400,000

    Cr. _____ . . . . _____

Inventory 1,400,000

RENT EXPENSE

5-45. Eastman Company will pay its December rent of $5,000 in January. In December 2001, it records the Rent Expense of December and the related liability, Accrued Rent, by the following journal entry:

Dr. _____ _____ .... _____

    Cr. _____ _____ ...... _____

Dr. Rent Expense 5,000

    Cr. Accrued Rent 5,000

5-46. In January 2002, Eastman Company paid $5,000 to its landlord for the December 2001 rent. The journal entry in January is:

Dr. _____ _____ .... _____

    Cr. _____ .... _____

Accrued Rent 5,000

    Cash 5,000

5-47. Earlier we saw that if rent is paid *prior* to the period in which the expense was incurred, the amount is first debited to Prepaid Rent, which is a(n) . . . [asset / liability] account. As the previous frame indicates, if rent is paid *after* the period in which the expense was incurred, the credit is made to Accrued Rent, which is a(n) . . . [asset / liability] account.

asset

liability

5-48. Prepaid Expenses are turned into expenses by a debit to the . . . [asset / expense] account and a credit to the . . . [asset / expense] account. Accrued Liabilities are discharged by a debit to . . . [Cash / Accrued Liabilities] and a credit to . . . [Cash / Accrued Liabilities].

expense   asset
Accrued Liabilities
Cash

5-49. Of course, many items of expense are paid for in cash during the accounting period. Salaries of $90,000 earned in 2001 and paid in cash in 2001 is recorded in the following entry.

Dr. _____ _____ .... _____

    Cr. _____ .... _____

Dr. Salary Expense 90,000

    Cr. Cash 90,000

6-49. In a **manufacturing** company, the cost of a finished product consists of three elements:

1. cost of materials used directly in that product;
2. cost of labor used directly on that product;
3. a fair share of overhead, or general costs associated with the production process.

Circle one word in each of 1, 2, and 3 above that best summarizes the whole phrase.

materials
labor
overhead

6-50. Some materials, such as oil for lubricating machinery, are not used directly in a product. The materials that are used *directly* in the product are called d _ _ _ _ _ materials. Similarly, the labor used directly to make the product is called _____ labor.

direct
direct

6-51. Production overhead consists of all other production costs, that is, costs that are not d _____ m _____ or d _____ l _____.

direct materials
direct labor

NOTE: In some manufacturing companies, computers and automated machine tools replace workers, so direct labor cost is relatively small. These companies combine labor costs and production overhead costs into a single item called **Other Production Costs.**

6-52. The three elements of production cost—**direct labor, direct materials,** and **overhead**—are added together to determine the total cost of the finished product. Until the product is sold, this amount is held in the Inventory account. When the product is sold, this amount becomes Cost of Sales. Thus, if a product requires $5 of direct labor, $7 of direct materials, and $3 of overhead, the product will be costed at $_____ as long as it is in the Inventory account. When it is sold, C _ _ _ of S _ _ _ _ will be $_____.

$15 (= $5 + $7 + $3)
Cost of
Sales $15

LOSSES

5-50. Assets provide benefits to future periods. Suppose Bryan Company owned an uninsured machine that was destroyed by fire in 2001. The machine . . . [will / will not] benefit future periods. The asset amount carried for the machine therefore expired in 2001, and this amount is recorded as an . . . [expense / expenditure] in 2001.

will not

expense

5-51. Thus, although an asset does not provide benefits during a period, it is an expense of that period if its cost has expired for any reason. Such expenses are called **losses.** A loss is recorded as an expense . . . [in the period in which the loss occurs / over the periods that the asset was supposed to benefit].

in the period in which the loss occurs

5-52. A loss is recorded as an expense if it is **reasonably possible** that the loss occurred, even though it is not certain. Thus, if a customer sues Bryan Company in 2001, and if it seems reasonably possible that Bryan Company will lose the law suit, the estimated loss is recorded as an expense . . . [in 2001 / when the law suit is settled]. This is in accordance with the concept that requires expenses to be recognized when they are reasonably possible, which is the c _ _ _ _ _ _ _ _ _ _ m concept.

in 2001

conservatism

SUMMARY OF MATCHING CONCEPT

5-53. Three types of costs are expenses of the current period. First, there are the costs of the goods and services that are **delivered** in the current period and whose r _ _ _ _ _ _ _ _ are recognized in that period.

revenues

> **NOTE:** The period in which revenues are recognized is determined first, according to the principles described in Part 4. Then the associated costs are matched with those revenues. Costs are matched against revenues, not vice versa.

6-44. In "writing down" inventory, the Inventory account is . . . [debited / credited], and Cost of Sales is . . . [debited / credited].

credited

debited

6-45. If inventory is written down by $20, what would the appropriate journal entry be?

Dr. _____ ____ _____   20

    Cr. _____   20

Cost of Sales   20

    Inventory   20

INVENTORY IN A MANUFACTURING COMPANY

6-46. Retail stores, wholesalers, and distributors are . . . [merchandising / manufacturing] companies. A company that makes shoes is a . . . [merchandising / manufacturing] company.

merchandising

manufacturing

6-47. A company that sells finished goods that it purchased from other vendors is a . . . [merchandising / manufacturing] company. A company that converts raw materials into finished goods and then sells these goods is a . . . [merchandising / manufacturing] company.

merchandising

manufacturing

6-48. A merchandising company buys its goods in salable form; it receives an invoice showing the cost for each item. The costs on these invoices are the amounts used to record the additions to inventory. A manufacturing company adds value to the raw material it buys; it must include these **conversion costs** in its inventory and in its cost of sales.

Measuring inventory and cost of sales is therefore more complicated in a . . . [merchandising / manufacturing] company.

manufacturing

5-54. Second, there are costs that are **associated with activities of the period.** The expenditures for these costs were made either in the current period or in an earlier period. If made in an earlier period, these amounts are a _____ on the balance sheet as of the beginning of the current period.

assets

5-55. Third, there are **losses** that are recognized in the current period. These may recognize a reasonably possible decrease in a(n) . . . [asset / liability] because of fire, theft, or other reasons. Or, they may recognize a reasonably possible increase in a(n) . . . [asset / liability] arising from events occurring in the period, such as a law suit.

asset

liability

5-56. The cash payments associated with any of these expenses may have been made in a prior period or in the current period, or they may be made in a future period, when the . . . [assets / liabilities] are paid.

liabilities

5-57. The balance sheet at the beginning of a period reports assets obtained as a result of e __ __ __ __ __ __ __ __ __ __ __ s made in earlier periods. Part of these asset amounts will expire and therefore will be e __ __ __ __ __ __ __ s of the current period. The remainder will be carried forward to future periods and will be reported as a __ __ __ __ __ __ on the balance sheet at the end of the current period.

expenditures

expenses

assets

NOTE: The next set of frames is an extended example of the use of the matching and realization concepts. If you now are comfortable with these concepts, skip to Frame 5-67. If you want additional practice, proceed with Frame 5-58.

6-39. In calculating income taxes, cost of sales is one of the items subtracted from revenue in order to find taxable income.

Assume that the revenue of Lewis Fuel Company was $1,000. Disregarding other expenses, if cost of sales was $470 (as in LIFO), LIFO taxable income would be $_____. If cost of sales was $400 (as in FIFO), FIFO taxable income would be $_____.

$530
$600

6-40. As can be seen from the above, the higher the cost of sales, the . . . [lower / higher] the taxable income. The lower the taxable income, the . . . [lower / higher] will be the income tax based on that income.

lower
lower

6-41. Companies usually prefer to pay as low an income tax as they legally can. Therefore, they prefer the method that results in the . . . [lower / higher] cost of sales. If prices are rising, this is usually the . . . [FIFO / LIFO] method.

higher
LIFO

> **NOTE:** Any of the methods described above is permitted in calculating taxable income in the United States. However, a company cannot switch back and forth between methods from one year to the next. In many countries, the LIFO method is not permitted. The method chosen by a company must be disclosed in the financial statements.

INVENTORY VALUATION: ADJUSTMENT TO MARKET

6-42. We have assumed so far that inventory is recorded at its cost. Suppose, however, that the fair value (i.e., market value) of the inventory falls below its original cost. The conservatism concept requires that we reduce the inventory account to the . . . [higher / lower] amount.

lower

6-43. For this reason, if the fair value of an item of inventory at the end of an accounting period is lower than its original cost, the item is "written down" to its f _____ v _____. For example, if an item whose original cost was $100 and whose current fair value is $80, its inventory amount should be written down by $_____. (This is an exception to the general rule that nonmonetary assets are reported at cost.)

fair value

$20 (= $100 − $80)

AN EXAMPLE OF MATCHING

> **NOTE:** Homes, Inc., is a company that buys and sells houses. Exhibit 7 in your booklet describes some of its transactions during May, June, and July. These events relate to the sale of two houses, House A and House B. We will measure the net income for Homes, Inc., for the month of June.

5-58. Delivery of the deed to a house is delivery of the ownership of the house. Exhibit 7 states that for House A this happened in _____ (what month?); therefore, revenue from the sale of House A is recognized in _____ (what month?).

June

June

5-59. The amount of revenue for House A is measured by two transactions. List these below and find the revenue for House A.

Date	Transaction*	Amount
May 2	_____ _____	$
June 5	_____	
	Revenue from House A	$

*Write a brief description of the transaction.

Date	Transaction	Amount
May 2	Down payment	$ 16,000
June 5	Payment	144,000
	Revenue from House A	$160,000

5-60. Now consider the costs that are associated with the total revenue from the sale of House A, $160,000, in June. One of these costs was the cost of House A, which was $_____.

$140,000

5-61. Two of the cash payments related specifically to the sale of House A. What were these cash decreases?

Date	Transaction	Amount
May ____	_____	$
July ____	_____	
	Total	$

Date	Transaction	Amount
May 15	Commission	$ 800
July 2	Commission	7,200
	Total	$8,000

6-34. In the LIFO section in Exhibit 9, enter the amount available for sale, $1,090; calculate the ending inventory; and subtract to find the cost of sales.

Goods available	$1,090
Ending inventory:	

	400 units @ $1.00 = $400	
	200 units @ $1.10 = _220_	
Total	600 units	620
Cost of sales		$ 470

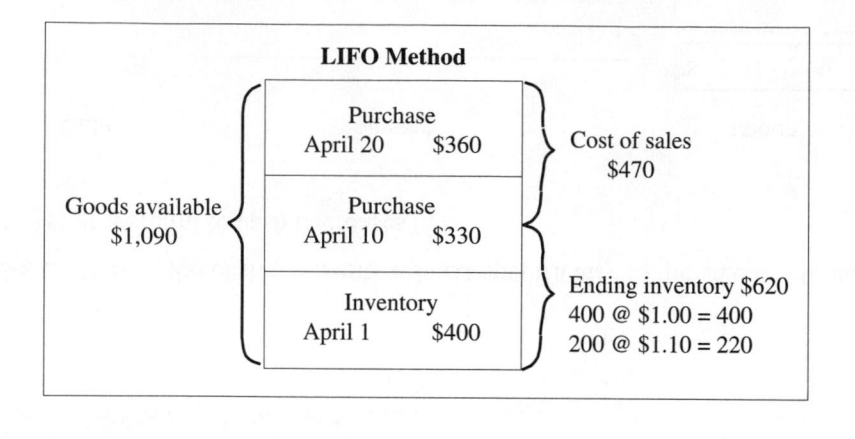

LIFO Method

Goods available $1,090

Purchase April 20 $360	Cost of sales $470
Purchase April 10 $330	
Inventory April 1 $400	Ending inventory $620 400 @ $1.00 = 400 200 @ $1.10 = 220

AVERAGE-COST METHOD

6-35. The third method is the **average-cost** method. It calculates the cost of both the ending inventory and the cost of sales at the average cost per unit of the goods available. In Exhibit 9, the number of units available in April was _____, and the total cost of these goods was $_____, so the average cost per unit was $_____.

1,000

$1,090 $1.09 (= $1,090 ÷ 1,000)

6-36. Using the average cost of $1.09 per unit, complete the average-cost section of Exhibit 9.

$\dfrac{\$1,090}{1,000}$ = $1.09 cost per unit

Ending inventory: 600 units @ $1.09 = $654
Cost of sales: 400 units @ $1.09 = $436

COMPARISON OF INVENTORY METHODS

6-37. Most businesses try to sell their oldest goods first, so the goods that were first out are likely to be the goods . . . [first in / last in]. The . . . [FIFO / LIFO] method reflects this practice.

first in

FIFO

6-38. From Exhibit 9, we see that cost of sales under FIFO was $_____, and under LIFO it was $_____. Cost of sales was . . . [lower / higher] under LIFO. In most companies, during periods of rising prices (i.e., inflation) this same relationship holds.

$400 $470

higher

5-62. The **matching** concept requires that the costs associated with the revenues of a period be recognized as expenses of that period. Therefore, the two commissions associated with House A, totaling $_____, should be recognized as expenses in _____ (what month?), even though they were not paid in that month.

$8,000   June

5-63. In accordance with the realization concept, the $24,000 down payment received on House B in June . . . [was / was not] revenue in June. It will be revenue in _____ (what month?). Because Homes, Inc., has an obligation to deliver the house, the $24,000 is a(n) . . . [asset / liability] on the balance sheet at the end of June.

was not

July

liability

5-64. The matching concept says that general costs of operations during any period are expenses of that period. Thus the $4,000 general costs of operations in June are expenses in _____ (what month?).

June

5-65. Refer to Frames 5-59 through 5-64 and complete the income statement for Homes, Inc., for the month of June, applying the realization concept and the matching concept.

HOMES, INC.

Income Statement for June

Sales Revenue	$ _____	$160,000 (= $16,000 + $144,000)
Expenses:		
Cost of House A	$ _____	$140,000
Commission Expense	_____	$8,000 (= $800 + $7,200)
General Expense	_____	4,000
Total Expense	_____	152,000
Net Income	$ _____	$8,000

6-31. Earlier, you found the amount of goods available for sale to be $1,090. Enter this amount in your calculation, and subtract the ending inventory of $690 from it. The difference is the FIFO c _____ of s _____ , which is $_____ .

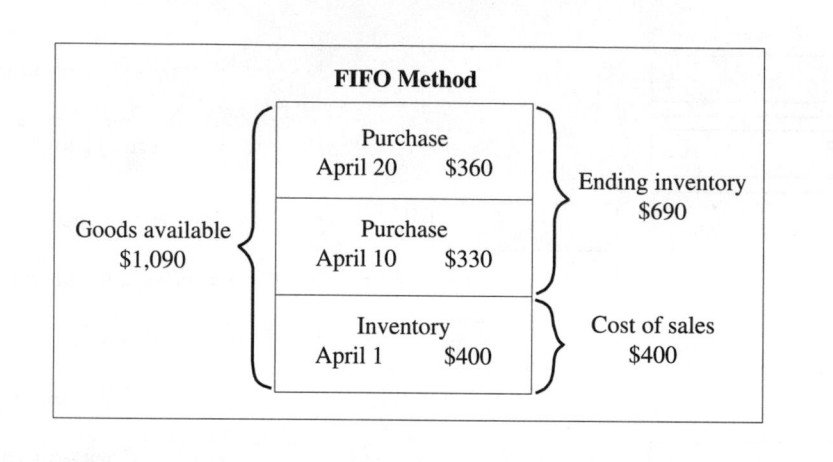

LAST-IN, FIRST-OUT (LIFO) METHOD

6-32. The FIFO method assumes that the oldest units—that is, those F _____ I _____ — were the first to be sold; that is, that they were the F _____ O _____ . The **LIFO** method assumes the opposite, namely, that the . . . [oldest / newest] units, which were the Last In, were the first to be sold; that is, that they were . . . [Last Out / First Out]; hence the name **Last-In First-Out.**

6-33. Because the LIFO method assumes that the last units purchased were the first ones to be sold, the ending inventory is assumed to consist of any remaining units in beginning inventory, plus the earliest units purchased. In Exhibit 9, the ending inventory was 600 units, and in the LIFO method these 600 units are assumed to be the _____ (how many?) units in beginning inventory plus _____ (how many?) of the 300 units purchased on April _____ .

5-66. According to Exhibit 7, cash transactions in June were:

June	Event	Cash Increases	Cash Decreases
2	Down payment on House B	$ 24,000	
5	Final payment on House A	144,000	
30	Commission on House B		$1,200
	General expenses for June		4,000

In June, Cash increased by a net amount of $_____. This increase . . . [was approximately the same as / had no relation to] the $8,000 net income for June.

THE INCOME STATEMENT

5-67. The equity section of a balance sheet shows the two sources of equity capital: (1) the capital supplied by equity investors (i.e., proprietors, partners, shareholders), which is called Paid-in C _ _ _ _ _ _ _ _ , and (2) that portion of the earnings resulting from profitable operations that have been retained in the entity, which is called R _ _ _ _ _ _ _ _ _ e _ _ _ _ _ _ _ _ _ .

5-68. The amount added to Retained Earnings as a result of profitable operations during a period is the **income** of the period. An i _ _ _ _ _ _ statement explains how this income was earned.

> **NOTE:** The income statement is also called a Profit and Loss, or Earnings, statement.

Homes, Inc.
INCOME STATEMENT, JUNE

Revenue	
May payment—A	$ 16,000
June payment—A	144,000
Total Revenue	160,000

Expenses	
Cost of house	140,000
May Commission—A	800
June Commission—A	7,200
June Expenses	4,000
Total expenses	152,000
Net Income	$ 8,000

$162,800 (= $168,000 − 5,200)

has no relation to

Capital

Retained earnings

income

6-26. The problem now is this: What unit cost should we assign to the ending inventory? There are three choices: (1) we could assume that the older fuel oil was sold, leaving the . . . [older / newer] fuel oil in inventory; (2) we could assume that the newer fuel oil was sold, leaving the . . . [older / newer] fuel in inventory; or (3) we could assume that a mixture of old and new oil was sold. Because the fuel oil has been mixed together in the storage tank, we . . . [have / do not have] a record of the cost of the specific quantities of fuel oil actually sold during the month. Therefore the solution . . . [is / is not] clearcut.

newer

older

do not have

is not

FIRST-IN, FIRST-OUT (FIFO) METHOD

6-27. In this situation, many companies make the **F**irst-**I**n **F**irst-**O**ut (**FIFO**) assumption, *for financial accounting purposes only.* They assume that the goods that came into the inventory . . . [first / last] are the . . . [first / last] to move out.

first
first

6-28. If you applied the FIFO method to the data of Exhibit 9, you would assume that the . . . [newer / older] fuel oil was sold during the month and that the . . . [newer / older] fuel oil remains in the ending inventory.

older
newer

6-29. The FIFO method assumes that the older units were sold during the period; therefore, the ending inventory of 600 units of fuel oil is assumed to be the most recently purchased fuel oil, namely, the 300 units purchased on April _____ at $_____ per unit and the 300 units purchased on April _____ at $_____ per unit.

20   $1.20

10   $1.10

6-30. In the "FIFO Method" section of Exhibit 9, enter these amounts and calculate the ending inventory.

Ending inventory

	300 units @ $1.20 = $360
	300 units @ $1.10 = 330
Total	600 units $690

5-69. There is no standard format for an income statement. The lower portion of Exhibit 8 shows one common format. The first item on this income statement is _____ _____, which is the amount of products (i.e., goods and services) _____ during the period.

Sales revenue

delivered to customers, or sold

5-70. The item on the second line is labeled _____ _____ _____. It reports the cost of the goods or services whose revenue is reported on the first line. This is an example of the _____ concept.

Cost of

sales

matching

5-71. The difference between sales and cost of sales is called _____ _____ in Exhibit 8. Write an equation, using the terms **cost of sales, sales revenue,** and **gross margin.**

Gross margin

_____ = _____ − _____

gross margin = sales revenue − cost
  of sales

5-72. Exhibit 8 shows that _____ _____ are subtracted from Gross margin, giving the item _____ _____ _____.

operating expenses

Income

before taxes

5-73. In accordance with the m _ _ _ _ _ _ _ _ concept, these expenses include costs related to the c _ _ _ _ _ _ _ period and costs that do not benefit f _ _ _ _ _ periods (i.e., losses).

matching

current

future

5-74. The next item on Exhibit 8, _____ _____ _____ _____, is shown separately because it is an especially important expense. These taxes relate to the income tax payable on the current period's income, not the income tax paid in that period.

Provision for

income taxes

5-75. The final item (the bottom line) on an income statement is called _____ _____ (or **net loss,** if expenses were larger than revenues).

Net income

INVENTORY VALUATION: ASSUMPTIONS

> **NOTE:** In the preceding frames, we assumed that all units of a given item, such as all Televisions #602, were purchased at the same time. Actually, the cost of goods purchased at different times may differ. For example, because inflation leads to increases in cost, the cost of goods purchased recently may be higher than the cost of the same goods purchased some time ago. In the following frames, we describe the three principal methods of finding cost of sales and ending inventory in such a situation.

6-22. Complete the following table, filling in all empty boxes.

	Quantity	Unit Cost	Total Cost
Beginning inventory, April 1	400	$1.00	$
Purchases, April 6	300	1.00	
Purchases, April 20	300	1.00	
Total goods available		1.00	
Ending inventory, April 30	600	1.00	
Cost of sales, April			

Quantity	Unit Cost	Total Cost
400	$1.00	$ 400
300	1.00	300
300	1.00	300
1,000	1.00	1,000
600	1.00	600
400	1.00	400

6-23. Lewis Fuel Company deals in fuel oil. Its inventory and purchases during April are shown in the top section of Exhibit 9 in the separate booklet. Fill in the two empty boxes in the column titled "Units."

Total goods available   1,000
Cost of sales, April   400

6-24. The "Unit Cost" column of Exhibit 9 shows that fuel oil entered the inventory at . . . [identical / different] unit costs during April.

different

6-25. In Exhibit 9 fill in the first four boxes in the column headed "Total Cost."

Units	Unit Cost	Total Cost
400	$1.00	$ 400
300	1.10	330
300	1.20	360
1,000		1,090

5-76. To arrive at net income, **dividends** . . . [are / are not] subtracted from revenues. Dividends . . . [are / are not] an expense. Dividends are a distribution of earnings to shareholders.

are not

are not

5-77. Revenues are defined as . . . [increases / decreases] in the _____ _____ item on the balance sheet. Expenses are . . . [increases / decreases] in that item. Net income is the difference between _____ and _____.

increases

Retained earnings

decreases

revenues   expenses

5-78. Because income is always supposed to be the *difference* between sales revenue and expenses, a term such as "sales income" . . . [is / is not] a misleading term. However, it is sometimes used.

is

A PACKAGE OF ACCOUNTING REPORTS

5-79. An income statement is a summary of R _____ e _____ that have been generated during a fiscal year.

Retained earnings

5-80. A(n) _____ _____ (what accounting report?) reports certain changes in Retained earnings that have taken place between two _____ _____ (what accounting reports?).

income statement

balance sheets

5-81. Thus, a useful accounting "report package" consists of a(n) _____ _____ at the beginning of the accounting period, a(n) _____ _____ for the period, and a(n) _____ _____ at the end of the period.

balance sheet

income statement

balance sheet

5-82. Exhibit 8 shows a financial report package consisting of an income statement and two balance sheets. Exhibit 8 shows that Retained earnings on December 31, 2001, was $_____.

$11,908,000

6-18. In the deduction method, goods not in inventory are assumed to have been sold. Sometimes goods are stolen, damaged, or spoiled. Therefore, the assumption that goods not in the closing inventory were sold . . . [is / is not] necessarily valid. However, steps are taken to discover and record this **shrinkage.**

is not

6-19. To summarize, many entities . . . [do / do not] keep track of individual items in inventory. They find their cost of sales by the process of **deduction.** This requires a . . . [perpetual / physical] inventory. An automobile dealership finds its cost of sales directly from its . . . [perpetual / physical] inventory records.

do not

physical
perpetual

6-20. Entities that must calculate cost of sales do so by subtracting the ending inventory from the total goods available, as in the following table:

	Cost ($000 omitted)			Cost ($000 omitted)
Beginning inventory	$ 200		Beginning inventory	$ 200
Purchases	600		Purchases	600
Total goods available			Total goods available	800
Ending inventory	300		Ending inventory	300
Cost of sales			Cost of sales	500

6-21. The same situation is shown in the following diagram. Fill in the boxes.

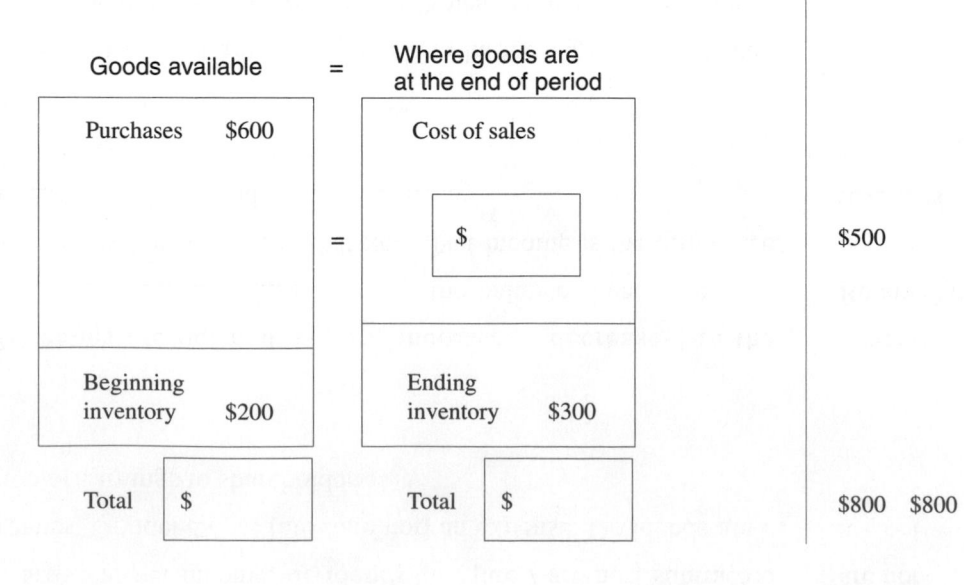

$500

$800 $800

5-83. During 2002, profitable operations resulted in net income of $_____$, which increased Retained earnings by this amount. (Net income is the **bottom line** on the income statement.)

$6,122,000

5-84. Retained earnings decreased by $4,390,000, representing a distribution to the shareholders in the form of _____.

dividends

5-85. As a result, the total Retained earnings on December 31, 2002, was $_____.

$13,640,000 (= $11,908,000 + $6,122,000 − $4,390,000)

5-86. Remember that dividends are . . . [an expense / a distribution of earnings to owners]. Dividends are *not*. . . . [an expense / a distribution of earnings to owners].

a distribution of earnings to owners
an expense

> **NOTE:** The "package" of required financial reports also includes a Statement of Cash Flows. This statement is described in Part 9.

INCOME STATEMENT PERCENTAGES

5-87. In an analysis of a business's performance, **percentages** of certain income statement items are usually calculated. The base (i.e., 100 percent) is **Sales revenue.** One percentage is the **gross margin percentage;** it is found by dividing G _ _ _ _ m _ _ _ _ _ _ by S _ _ _ _ _ r _ _ _ _ _ _ _ .

Gross margin
Sales revenue

5-88. Calculate the gross margin percentage for Garsden Company in 2002.

$$\frac{\text{Gross margin} \quad \boxed{\$ \qquad}}{\text{Sales revenue} \quad \boxed{\$ \qquad}} = \boxed{} \%*$$

$$\frac{\$23,251}{\$75,478} = 31\%$$

_____
*Show the nearest percent.

6-13. Therefore, the **goods available for sale** in a period are the sum of the b _____ inventory plus the p _____ during the period.

beginning   purchases

6-14. On January 1, 2001, Cantal Hardware had an inventory that cost $200,000. During 2001 it purchased $600,000 of additional merchandise. The cost of goods **available for sale** in 2001 was $_____.

$800,000 (= $200,000 + $600,000)

6-15. Accountants *assume* that goods available for sale during a period either are in inventory at the end of the period or were sold. Thus, if goods costing $800,000 were available for sale during 2001 and goods costing $300,000 were in inventory on December 31, 2001, cost of sales in 2001 is **assumed** to be $_____.

$500,000 (= $800,000 − $300,000)

6-16. At the end of each accounting period, all goods currently on hand are counted. This process is called **taking a physical inventory.** Since its purpose is to find the cost of the goods that were sold, each item is reported at its . . . [cost / selling price].

cost

6-17. In order to determine the ending inventory of one period and the beginning inventory of the next period, how many physical inventories must be taken? _____

One (*because the ending inventory on December 31, 2001 is also the beginning inventory on January 1, 2002*)

NOTE: Entities that use the perpetual inventory method count physical inventory at least annually. This inventory may reveal that the actual ending inventory is lower than is indicated in the perpetual inventory records because of theft, errors in record keeping, or items that have been discarded. If so, the ending inventory is reduced by a credit entry. The offsetting debit entry is to an expense account, Loss on Inventory.

5-89. An even more important percentage is the **Net income percentage.** Calculate it for Garsden Company.

Net income $ [____]

————————— = ——————————————— = [___] %*

Sales revenue $ [____]

————————

*Show the nearest percent.

$$\frac{\$\ 6{,}122}{\$75{,}478} = 8\%$$

> **NOTE:** The net income of many American manufacturing corporations is roughly 5% to 10% of sales revenue, but there is a wide variation among companies.

REVIEW OF BASIC CONCEPTS

> The nine basic concepts described in this program are listed in the following frames, together with some guides that will refresh your memory of their meaning. Complete the meaning of each concept. (These concepts are not stated as such in accounting literature, but most accountants would agree that they are the basic underpinnings of accounting.)

5-90. Dual-aspect concept: _____ = _____ + _____.

Assets = Liabilities + Equity
(See frames 1-16 to 1-22.)

5-91. Money-measurement concept: Accounting reports only facts that can be expressed _____.

in monetary amounts
(If you have the general idea, fine. Your words need not be exactly like those given here.)
(See frames 1-27 to 1-33.)

5-92. Entity concept: Accounts are kept for an _____ as distinguished from the p _ _ _ _ _ _ _ associated with that entity.

entity

persons
(See frames 1-34 to 1-39.)

5-93. The accounting concept that assumes that an entity will continue to operate indefinitely and that it is not about to be sold is the g _ _ _ _ _ -c _ _ _ _ _ _ concept.

going-concern
(See frames 1-40 to 1-43.)

6-8. Televisions that cost $1,800 were sold in May for $2,500. Complete the following partial income statement, assuming these were the only items sold.

Income Statement
May

Sales revenue	$
Cost of sales	
Gross margin	$

Income Statement
May

Sales revenue	$2,500
Cost of sales	1,800
Gross margin	$ 700

FINDING COST OF SALES BY DEDUCTION

6-9. If an entity has a p _____ inventory, as illustrated above, finding cost of sales in a month is easy. We shall next show how to deduce cost of sales in a business that does not have this record. This method is the process of **deduction.**

perpetual

6-10. Many stores, such as hardware stores, carry so many relatively low-value items that keeping a perpetual inventory record for each separate item is not practical. When the salesperson rings up a sale on the cash register, a record is made of the . . . [cost of sales / sales revenue] but not the . . . [cost of sales / sales revenue].

sales revenue

cost of sales

> **NOTE:** With computers, many more companies use the perpetual inventory method. The cash register (point-of-sale terminal) then records both sales revenue and the cost of sales.

6-11. If a hardware store does not keep a record of the cost of each item in inventory, it . . . [can arrive at cost of sales directly / must deduce cost of sales by an indirect method].

must deduce cost of sales by an indirect method

6-12. Items in a hardware store's **beginning inventory** on January 1, 2001 . . . [are / are not] available for sale during 2001. Additional items **purchased** and placed on the shelves during 2001 . . . [are / are not] available for sale during 2001.

are

are

5-94. Asset-measurement concept: Accounting focuses on the f _ _ _ _ v _ _ _ _ _ of monetary assets; nonmonetary assets are reported at an amount based on c _ _ _ _ .

fair value

cost
(See frames 1-44 to 1-57.)

5-95. Conservatism concept: Revenues are recognized when they are reasonably c _ _ _ _ _ _ _ . Expenses are recognized when they are reasonably p _ _ _ _ _ _ _ .

certain

possible
(See frames 4-18 to 4-22.)

5-96. Materiality concept: Disregard _____ matters.

immaterial (or insignificant)

Disclose _____ matters.

all important
(See frames 4-23 to 4-30.)

5-97. Realization concept: Revenues are recognized when goods or services are _____ .

delivered
(See frames 4-31 to 4-51.)

5-98. The **mat** _ _ _ _ _ _ **concept** states that the expenses of a period are costs associated with the revenues or activities of the period.

matching
(See frames 5-19 to 5-23.)

KEY POINTS TO REMEMBER

- Expenditures are made when goods or services are acquired. If these goods or services are used up during the current period, they are expenses of the period. If not used up, they are assets at the end of that period. These assets will become expenses in future periods as they are used up.

- Some expenditures result in liabilities that will be paid in future periods. An example is accrued salaries.

- Expenses are expired costs. Assets are unexpired costs.

- Matching concept: Costs associated with the revenues or activities of a period are expenses of the period.

- Expenses of a period are (1) cost of the products (i.e., goods and services) that were delivered to customers during the period; (2) other expenditures that benefit operations of the period; and (3) losses, that is, decreases in assets from fire, theft, and other unusual reasons, and increases in liabilities from unusual events, such as lawsuits.

This is called a **perpetual inventory** record. "Receipts" are . . . [increases / decreases] in inventory, and "Shipments to Customers" are . . . [increases / decreases] in inventory.

increases

decreases

6-6. Information in the perpetual inventory records corresponds to that in the Inventory account. From the previous frame, we see that the beginning balance for Television #602 in the Inventory account on May 1 was $_____. There were receipts during May of $_____, which added to Inventory; these were . . . [Dr. / Cr.] to the Inventory account. Shipments during May decreased inventory by $_____, which were . . . [Dr. / Cr.] to the Inventory account. This decrease in inventory was Cost of Sales in May, which was $_____.

$800 $2,000

Dr.

$1,800

Cr.

$1,800

6-7. Using the *totals* in the perpetual inventory record, enter the inventory transactions for May in the T-accounts given below. (The inventory purchases were on credit.)

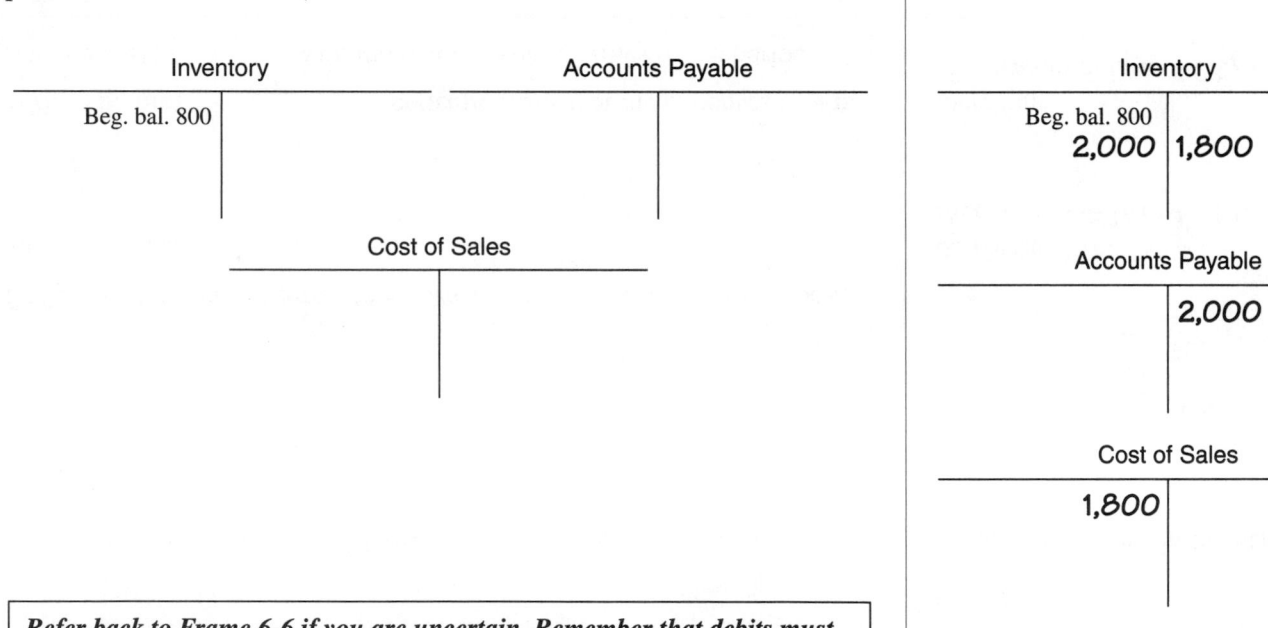

	Inventory			Accounts Payable	
Beg. bal. 800					

	Cost of Sales	

	Inventory	
Beg. bal. 800		
2,000	1,800	

	Accounts Payable	
	2,000	

	Cost of Sales	
1,800		

> *Refer back to Frame 6-6 if you are uncertain. Remember that debits must equal credits.*

- The income statement summarizes revenues and expenses of the period. Its "bottom line," or net income, shows the increase in equity resulting from activities during the period.

- Dividends are a distribution of earnings to shareholders. Dividends are not expenses.

- Retained earnings at the beginning of the period + Net Income − Dividends = Retained Earnings at the end of the period.

- Percentages are calculated for various income statement items, especially gross margin and net income, taking sales revenue as 100 percent.

You have completed Part 5 of this program. If you think you understand the material in this part, you should now take Post Test 5, which is in the separate booklet. If you are uncertain about your understanding, you should review Part 5.

The post test will serve both to test your comprehension and to review the highlights of Part 5. After taking the post test, you may find that you are unsure about certain points. You should review these points before going on to Part 6.

6-2. In some entities, matching cost of sales and sales revenue is easy. For example, an automobile dealer keeps a record of the cost of each automobile in its inventory. If the dealer sold two automobiles during a given month, one for $18,000 that had cost $16,000, and the other for $10,000 that had cost $7,500, sales revenue for the period would be recorded as $_____ and cost of sales as $_____. This is the **specific identification** method.

$28,000 (= $18,000 +$10,000)
$23,500 (= $16,000 + $7,500)

6-3. A dealer sold an automobile costing $16,000 for $18,000 cash. Write the journal entry that records the effect of this transaction solely on the Sales Revenue and Cash accounts:

Dr. _____ .... _____

    Cr. _____ _____ ... _____

Cash 18,000
    Sales Revenue   18,000

6-4. A dealer sold an automobile costing $16,000 for $18,000 cash. Write the journal entry that records the effect of this transaction solely on the Inventory and Cost of Sales accounts:

Dr. _____ ____ _____ .... _____

    Cr. _____ .... _____

Cost of Sales 16,000
    Inventory   16,000

6-5. A dealer that sells televisions might keep a record of its inventory of each type of television, something like the following:

Item: Television #602, Cost $200 each

Date	Receipts		Shipments to Customers		On Hand	
	Quantity	Cost	Quantity	Cost	Quantity	Cost
May 1					4	800
6			1	200	3	600
10	10	2,000			13	2,600
13			6	1,200	7	1,400
31			2	400	5	1,000
Totals	10	2,000	9	1,800	5	1,000

Part 6

Inventories and Cost of Sales

Learning Objectives

In this part you will learn:

• How the cost of sales is calculated.

• Methods of arriving at inventory amounts.

• When inventory amounts on the balance sheet are reduced.

• How inventory is measured in a manufacturing company.

• The distinction between product costs and period costs.

• How overhead rates are calculated.

FINDING COST OF SALES

6-1. In the income statement in Part 5, the first item subtracted from sales revenue was called **Cost of sales.** It is the cost of the same products whose revenues are included in the sales amount. This is an example of the m _ _ _ _ _ _ _ _ concept. (Some businesses call this item **Cost of goods sold.**) In most businesses the cost of sales is the . . . [smallest / largest] item of expense, amounting to as much as 85% of sales revenues in a profitable supermarket and 60–70% in a profitable manufacturing company.

matching

largest